Caring IN A Crisis

What to do and who to turn to

Marina Lewycka

To my mother Halyna Lewycka,
and all those who cared for her.

©1993 Marina Lewycka
Published by Age Concern England
1268 London Road
London SW16 4ER

Editor Caroline Hartnell
Production Marion Peat
Design and typesetting Eugenie Dodd
Printed in Great Britain by Bell and Bain Ltd, Glasgow

A catalogue record for this book is available from the British Library.

ISBN 0–86242–136–5

Contents

About the author

Marina Lewycka is a lecturer and freelance writer. She contributed to the BBC handbook *Who Cares Now?*, and her training resource pack *Survival Skills for Carers* is published by the National Extension College with support from the Department of Health. She has been involved in the organisation of weekend courses for carers.

Acknowledgements

Many people have contributed their ideas and experience to this book. In particular I would like to thank Lee Bennett for her initial encouragement and David Moncrieff and Marion Peat for their continuing advice and support. I would like to thank Evelyn McEwen, Barbara Meredith, David Bookbinder, Sally West, Audrey King and Jane Whelan for their helpful comments on the text, Vinnette Marshall for her meticulous work on the copy, and above all Caroline Hartnell for her sympathetic and painstaking editing.

I am deeply grateful to the many people here in Sheffield in the health service, the local authority housing and social services departments, voluntary organisations, and the Royal College of Nursing, who answered my many awkward questions so patiently, and to Gilda Petersen and Alison Leapish for their help and constructive advice.

Finally I would like to thank the people who spoke to me so openly about their own situations. Their willingness to share their experiences has not only enriched the book, but will I hope be a source of practical wisdom and comfort to other people in a time of crisis.

Introduction

Most of us have to look after an older relative at some time in our lives. It often happens when we are least prepared. We may be so busy with our own jobs and families that it's easy to forget that our parents are getting older. Besides, they always seem to cope so well. Then suddenly something happens – an accident or an illness – and their world and ours is turned upside down.

If the person who needs care lives many miles away, it can be difficult to know whom to contact and where to get help. Families nowadays often live far apart, and making arrangements at a distance can be an extra problem.

This book aims to help you through those first hours and days. It explains the roles of the professional workers who will look after your relative, and looks at the decisions you may have to make. It also looks at some longer-term options for the care of your relative, and the services which may be available.

The book is for anyone who suddenly finds themselves having to look after another person. That other person is perhaps most likely to be one of our parents, or a partner. But many people also find themselves looking after grandparents, an uncle or aunt, a brother or sister, or a close friend who suddenly becomes ill or has an accident. Although the book talks about caring for a relative, you do not of course have to be related to someone to care for them.

The person being cared for is referred to as 'she' throughout the book because there are more older women than older men so a person needing care is more likely to be a woman.

1 Dealing with a crisis

In the past it was usually a telegram that brought bad news. Nowadays it is more likely to be a telephone call that alerts you to a crisis. It might be a call from a relative or a neighbour, or from the hospital where your relative has been admitted.

Your relative may have fallen ill, or had an accident. Or a long-standing condition such as cancer or Alzheimer's disease may have become suddenly worse. Or the person who usually looks after her may have fallen ill or had an accident, leaving her on her own. What should you do?

Your first reaction may well be one of panic, especially if the call is unexpected or comes late at night. However upset you feel, try to keep calm. It will help you think more clearly. People have different ways of calming themselves down. You could try some of the techniques suggested in the box on pages 9–10.

JULIE

'It was six o'clock one evening when I heard about my mother's accident. I was just getting the tea on the table. Peter had got back late and tired from work. The twins were demanding attention. It was one of those days. Then there was this phone call from the hospital in Cleveland, saying my mother had had a bad fall, and had broken her leg.

'I just panicked. "Right," I said, "I'm off! I've got to get up there. I'm bringing her back with me. She can't go on living alone."

'Peter calmed me down. "Sit down," he said, "and finish your tea. Let's talk this through. I've got nothing against your mother living with us, if it's the best thing for everybody. But we can't just rush into a big decision like this."

'Over tea, we talked through the possibilities. Peter said, "Why don't you phone your brother in Newcastle. It's much nearer for him. He could go up tonight, and you can go up tomorrow."

'I phoned my brother. He'd also heard from the hospital, and was just about to set off. "I'll be there in half an hour," he said, "but I can't stay next day, because of work." I said I would go up next day, and we agreed that we'd get together later on and have a talk. I arranged for a neighbour to pick the twins up from school next day, and I went up on the train.

'I was glad I phoned my brother. I'd never been very close to him, and somehow I didn't think he'd be much help. In fact looking after mother has brought us closer together, and now we share caring for her.'

TIPS FOR KEEPING CALM

▶ Take slow, deep breaths into the lower part of your stomach, and breathe out with a sigh. Put your hand on your stomach below the waist, and feel it go up and down as you breathe.

▶ Count backwards from ten, breathing out deeply with a sigh on each count. (Again, breathe into the lower part of your stomach.)

- ▶ Go for a brisk walk round the block.
- ▶ Make yourself a drink.
- ▶ Find someone to talk to.
- ▶ Ring one of the helplines on pages 107–120.

Deciding what to do now and what can wait

If your relative, or the person who looks after her, is injured or seriously ill, there may be major decisions to be made about where she will live and how she will be cared for. But you do not have to make all these decisions immediately. In fact, it is better to leave the big decisions until her condition has stabilised, and you have a clearer picture of how much care she will need.

Waiting a bit also gives you time to adjust to the situation. When you first see your relative, especially if she is in hospital, you may feel quite shocked and upset. It is best to try not to let this show, and remind yourself that this is a crisis, and that things can change very quickly. She may begin to look much better after she has rested for a day or two in hospital.

The long-term decisions are looked at in Chapter 5. It is best to take your time making these decisions, and to talk to everyone who could be affected, as it is easy to make the wrong decision under pressure, and then regret it.

Assessing the immediate situation

There are certain decisions you will need to make immediately: Will your relative be all right on her own until you arrive or do you need to arrange for someone to sit with her until you get there? Is the situation so serious that an ambulance needs to be called? If your relative (or her carer) has had a fall or been taken suddenly ill, you will in any case want to be sure that the GP has been contacted.

Before you can make any decision, you will need to find out as much as possible about your relative's condition. When you got the initial phone call alerting you to the crisis, whether from your relative herself or from a neighbour or even from her GP, you may well have been too shocked to ask all the questions you should have. In this case it is vital to ring back and find out more. The following are some of the questions you might want to ask:

▶ Has the doctor been called?

▶ If the doctor has not been called, can your relative do it herself or should you do it? Doctor's phone number?

▶ Can your relative get up from her chair or her bed – to go to the toilet, or to make herself a hot drink? And to answer the door when the doctor comes?

▶ Is there a neighbour who could be asked to come round? Has the neighbour got a key?

▶ Is she feeling dizzy, breathless, drowsy or in pain?

▶ If your relative has had a fall, is she bleeding anywhere? Does she think she has broken a bone? Can she move the affected part of her body?

▶ Does she feel worried about being on her own until you arrive?

If your relative cannot answer the door herself and there isn't anyone else who has a key and can come round, the doctor will contact the police and they will break in to your relative's home.

If it is a neighbour or the GP you speak to rather than your relative, some of these questions will obviously not need to be asked. The very fact that someone else is already with your relative will make the situation a bit less alarming for you.

The crisis flow-chart on pages 12–13 should help guide you through the things you have to do now. If you decide you do have to arrange emergency care for your relative, see pages 14–15 for suggestions about whom to contact.

Crisis flow-chart

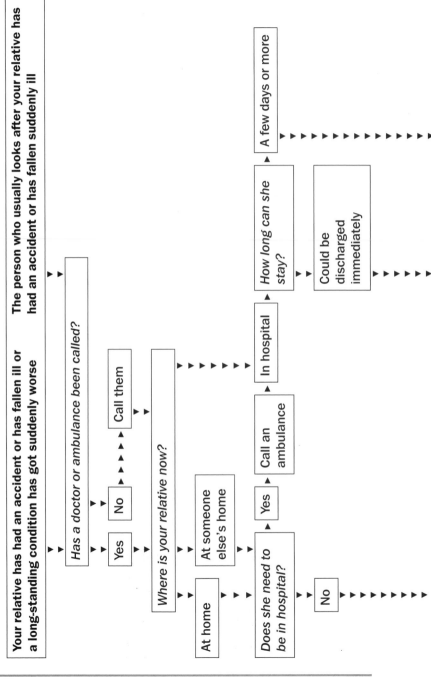

Your relative has had an accident or has fallen ill or a long-standing condition has got suddenly worse

The person who usually looks after your relative has had an accident or has fallen suddenly ill

Has a doctor or ambulance been called?

Yes

No → Call them

Where is your relative now?

At home

At someone else's home

Does she need to be in hospital?

Yes → Call an ambulance → In hospital

No

How long can she stay?

A few days or more

Could be discharged immediately

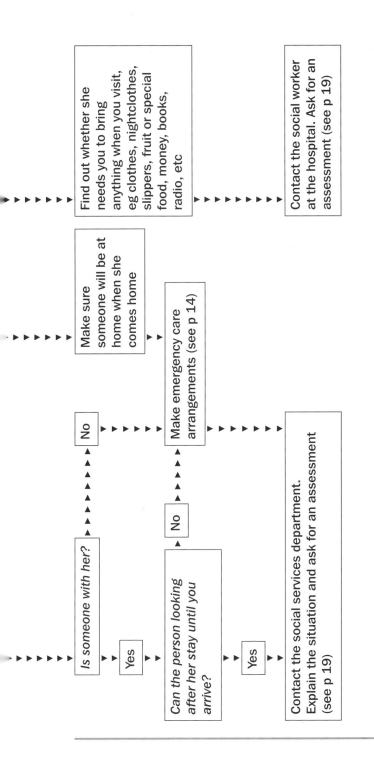

Arranging care in an emergency

When you hear of your relative's crisis, you may be able to just drop everything and go to her. But for some people, this is just not possible. Or you may have other commitments, which mean that you cannot stay for very long. In either case, you will need to arrange short-term emergency care, until more permanent arrangements can be made.

Listed below are some suggestions for whom to contact if you need to arrange care for your relative at very short notice. (Chapter 3 looks in more detail at who's who in the local authority and the health service.) If you live some distance away, or do not know the relevant phone numbers, you may need to go through Directory Enquiries to contact them.

Whom to contact

Other members of your family who live near your relative.

A friend or neighbour of your relative who lives close by.

Your relative's GP.

The district nurse (this may be difficult if it is a weekend).

The social services department in your relative's area. They may be able to do an emergency assessment (see pp 19–21) or arrange temporary care at short notice. Ask for the duty officer and explain the situation, saying that your relative needs immediate care. There should be a 24-hour emergency number.

The hospital social worker (if your relative is in hospital, but may be discharged shortly). Explain that there may be no one to look after your relative when she returns home.

The Crossroads Care Attendant scheme in your relative's area. This is a national charity which provides respite care in people's homes, and may also provide emergency care. The service is free, but there are different criteria in different areas for who can qualify. Sometimes Crossroads can be contracted by the local social services department to provide emergency care.

A private agency such as Care Alternatives in the London area (address on p 109), which provides care for elderly people in their own homes and may be able to arrange for someone to sit with your relative until you arrive. Fees may be expensive – from £7 per hour. The United Kingdom Home Care Association (address on p 119) should be able to tell you about similar agencies in other parts of the country.

The local branch of Age Concern in your relative's area. They will know about any other voluntary, private or council-run care services in the area. They may also have a network of volunteer visitors who will drop in.

A nursing agency (look in the *Yellow Pages*). They can provide a trained nurse to go into your relative's home. Fees can vary from £5 to £20 per hour, depending where you live.

An agency already known to your relative, for example a church or voluntary group, from which she may already be receiving support.

The ambulance service, if you think your relative may need hospital care.

The police If you cannot contact anyone else, ring the police in your relative's area, and explain the situation to them. They will know the local social services emergency procedure, and they will arrange an ambulance if necessary.

Finding out more about your relative's illness or disability

There will almost certainly be a voluntary group or charity which offers advice and information about your relative's illness or disability (see the list of useful organisations on pp 107–120).

Most of these charities or voluntary organisations are national – that is, they cover the whole country – but sometimes there are also local branches. These will be listed in your telephone directory, or the national office will be able to put you in touch with local contacts.

Other people who can help

It is all too easy to feel that everything is up to you, and that you have to solve all the problems single-handed. In fact, of course, you are not on your own. Apart from other members of the family and friends, there are other people whose job it is to help, and to whom you can turn for advice and support.

Health care staff
Your relative's GP
Your own GP (if you are feeling very stressed)
District nurse
Community psychiatric nurse
Hospital nursing staff

Social services
Social worker
Home care organiser
Officer in charge of residential or nursing home

Voluntary organisations
Age Concern
Help the Aged

Local church
Local community group
Local Good Neighbour or befriending scheme
Carers National Association
Club or society to which your relative belongs or belonged
Welfare association or trade union connected with your relative's employment

Other people you know

_____

_____

_____

_____

You could ask the local Council for Voluntary Service or the Community Health Council if they know about other voluntary or self-help groups in your area.

Don't be afraid or embarrassed to ask for help. People who support carers know what a difficult and sometimes lonely task you face, and they will be only too pleased to help.

2 Arranging care for your relative

This section looks at how to make arrangements for your relative's care once you have made sure she is safe, and the most immediate crisis is past. If you have not already contacted the local social services department, it may be a good idea to involve them now, to help you make whatever arrangements are necessary. When phoning social services, it is often difficult to find out whom you should be speaking to. Chapter 3 explains how social services departments are organised.

Some people are reluctant to contact social services. They think social workers are for other people, so-called 'problem families', or people with serious disabilities. They think that families should 'look after their own'. While pride and independence are very valuable qualities – a source of strength which helps many elderly people to keep going – they can sometimes make things unnecessarily difficult. Remember your relative or her spouse has probably been paying taxes for years, so they have earned their right to be looked after in their time of need.

KEN

Ken's father went to live with Ken and Ella and their two sons when his wife died. He had had a stroke, and could only get about with difficulty. He needed a lot of looking after, including help with washing and dressing. 'Well, we didn't mind that. The problem was, Dad wouldn't let anyone apart from me and Ella do anything for him. But we were both working, and we found we just weren't giving enough time to the kids – or to each other. The social worker said we should get somebody in to help. She said they had people who would come to the house and help him with personal care. But he said, "I don't want any strangers looking after me."

'We struggled on for a bit longer, and then Ella said she just couldn't cope any more. She said either he has someone come here to look after him, or he goes into a home. So Dad agreed, and social services sent somebody round. We thought she was really nice, but after the first time she came round Dad said she'd stolen some money, and he wouldn't have her in the house. We had a big row.

'The social worker suggested that Dad could go into a home just for a couple of weeks, to give me and Ella a break. But Dad refused to go. He said we were abandoning him. I couldn't really argue with him. He just made me feel so guilty. Then the social worker tried to talk to him, but he wouldn't listen to her either. He said she was interfering.

'In the end it was the GP who persuaded Dad to go into respite care. He explained that looking after him was a full-time job for us, and we needed a holiday. I don't know why, but Dad accepted that – maybe because the GP was a man, or maybe because he was nearer Dad's age. I think the GP pointed out that if we couldn't cope, then he might have to go into a home permanently.

'In fact he really enjoyed his two weeks away, and he talks about it all the time. You can't imagine what a difference it made to us, that two weeks' holiday.'

Now the GP has also persuaded Ken's father to let someone get him up and dress him a couple of mornings a week, and put him to bed in the evening.

Assessing your relative's needs

If your relative wants to stay at home but needs help in order to manage (or if she wants to go into a care home but needs help with the cost), the local social services department should carry out an **assessment**. Under the NHS and Community Care Act 1990, which came into force in April 1993, councils have a duty to assess the needs of people who appear to need community care services.

The aim of the assessment is to identify your relative's needs and then to make a decision about what, if anything, the social services department will do to help. If it is decided that the social services department will provide or arrange services, she will have a financial assessment to see how much she should pay towards the cost of care.

You can ask the local social services department to carry out an assessment for your relative. Just ring up and ask for the duty officer and explain what you want. They should pass on your details to the right person, or tell you whom to contact. This may well be the team leader or service manager for the area where your relative lives (see pp 35–36 for an explanation of how social services departments are organised).

All local councils have different ways of arranging assessments. In some places there are specially trained assessors. In others the assessment may be done by someone like a social worker, an occupational therapist or a home care organiser (see pp 36–37 on the roles of the different people who make up the social services team).

If your relative is in hospital, you should contact the social work department at the hospital and say that you would like your relative to be assessed so that she can get the help she needs when she is discharged.

If you are able to organise help at home for your relative yourself, and you and/or your relative are able to pay for it, there is no need to involve the social services department. But it may still be worth doing, because you may find out about other services for your relative which you had not thought of.

What questions will be asked?

The way the assessment is done will depend on how much help your relative needs and on how the social services department in your relative's area is organised. Someone who just needs, say, some help with cleaning at home will have a less detailed assessment than someone who is severely disabled and needs a lot of care. A simple assessment might involve just a few questions over the phone. If there are health needs, the person carrying out the assessment must ask the opinion of a doctor or nurse as well (probably your relative's GP, district nurse or health visitor, or a hospital doctor).

If your relative has a full assessment, the person doing it should ask about:

Biographical details Age, family circumstances, ethnic origin, religion, etc.

What help your relative thinks she needs.

How well she can manage Can she look after herself, and cope with everyday tasks such as getting washed and dressed, eating, walking around, going up and down stairs?

Her health, both physical and mental They may consult the doctor at the hospital, or your relative's GP, health visitor or district nurse for more information.

Medicines Does your relative need to take medicines regularly, and does this cause any problems?

Lifestyle, abilities, culture, ethnic background and personal factors such as bereavement: how do these affect your relative's view of her situation and her ability to cope?

Whether there is a carer A carer has a right to be consulted as well, and if necessary to have their own needs assessed.

Who else is around to help Friends, neighbours, other family members, etc.

What help she is getting already From social services or other agencies.

Her housing situation Does your relative want to stay where she is? If so, does the house need to be adapted in any way? Or is she considering moving into sheltered housing or a residential or nursing home?

Transport Does your relative have difficulty in getting to the shops, doctor, etc?

Whether she is at risk Does she suffer from an illness which might cause her to collapse suddenly, for example diabetes, epilepsy or heart failure? Has she had a number of falls or other accidents or 'near misses' at home? Does she perhaps put others at risk by strange, threatening or erratic behaviour? (Sometimes people with Alzheimer's disease turn on the gas and then forget to light it – a risk both to themselves and to neighbours.)

Finance What income and savings does your relative have, and what benefits is she claiming? They may ask for proof, such as pension books, or bank or building society statements. They will probably try to make sure that your relative is claiming all the benefits she is entitled to.

It is always a good idea to ask for a written record of the assessment. If you are not satisfied with the assessment, you can ask for a review, using the social services department's **complaints procedure**. You may feel that the assessment has not been carried out properly – it may have consisted of no more than a few questions asked over the phone – and that your relative has not had a chance to express her needs. Or you may feel that the services offered do not adequately meet her assessed needs, as discussed below.

All social services departments must now have a complaints procedure. People should be told about it when their needs are being assessed, but this may not happen, particularly if they are assessed over the phone.

Meeting your relative's needs

Once your relative's needs have been assessed, the social services department will decide whether they can offer help. If they do decide to help, the next step will be to arrange care services for your relative. The services offered should meet her assessed needs. In practice some local authorities may say they do not have enough money to meet everybody's needs.

Particularly if her needs are complex, your relative should in theory be offered services in the form of a 'care plan', which sets out in writing what services are being offered, what this is supposed to achieve, when her needs will be reviewed, and whether she appears to need other services such as health services. In practice this does not seem to happen very often, but it is always a good idea to ask the social services department to give you this information in writing.

If you feel that what the social services department is offering is inadequate to meet your relative's needs, you can make a complaint, using the complaints procedure. Social services may, for example, offer to send someone in every morning to help her get up, but your relative may feel she can't manage without help in the evening as well. If you appeal against the decision, but further help is still refused, you may in the end find you have to arrange – and pay for – the extra care yourselves.

However, you may wish at the same time to continue to pursue the matter further through legal or other means. Further advice on how to go about this is available from Age Concern England. National organisations such as the Carers National Association or the Alzheimer's Disease Society (addresses on pp 109 and 107) may also be able to advise you.

Listed on pages 26–29 are some of the services which could be offered if the social services department does decide to help your relative. This could include a temporary convalescent stay in a residential or nursing home, as explained on page 25.

Although the services may be organised by the social services department, they may not all be provided by them. Some may be provided by private agencies, or by voluntary organisations such as Crossroads or Age Concern. The social services department should contact all the different people involved in providing services for your relative.

If the person doing the assessment finds there is a health problem that your relative's GP does not know about, they should inform the GP or district nurse, with your relative's permission.

SOPHIE

6 At first they were a bit overwhelmed at having so many different people coming round all the time. 9

Sophie's mother was admitted to hospital when she collapsed with heart failure. After about a fortnight she was ready to go home. But there was no one to look after her apart from her husband, also in his 80s. Although he was very willing, he didn't seem to have what it takes to be a full-time carer.

'Dad is a bit forgetful, he often falls asleep during the afternoon, and I don't think he has ever cooked a meal in his life. Fortunately social services were very understanding – I think maybe more than if it had been the other way round, and it was Mum caring for Dad.

'At first I was worried that nothing seemed to be happening. The social worker at the hospital seemed to be so busy, it was hard to get to talk to her. We didn't even realise Mum had been assessed – it just seemed as though they had come round for a chat. In fact the services have been excellent. When we hear what other people have had to put up with, we realise how lucky we've been.

'There were problems about Mum going home. She couldn't manage the stairs, and there was no bathroom or toilet downstairs. The occupational therapist from the hospital had been round before Mum was discharged, to talk about the arrangements and make sure she would be able to manage. Now the social services occupational therapist came round and recommended they had a stair lift put in. She said they could get a grant towards the cost. The lady from Care and Repair came round and explained about the grant.

'In the meantime, social services arranged for someone to come in the morning and give her a wash, and help her get dressed. And someone else comes in the evening and helps her get to bed. There is also a home help twice a week – the service is run by Age Concern on contract to the council. She has to pay a flat fee for the personal care, and the home help is charged at an hourly rate, but they are both very reasonable. Someone from a voluntary organisation called Share the Care comes and sits with her for an hour in the afternoon, and she also has a voluntary visitor from Age Concern.

'The district nurse has sorted out a wheelchair for her, so we can take her for walks round the block. And the occupational therapist came with a special raised toilet seat, and a frame round the toilet that bolts to the floor, so she can pull herself up.

'They can have meals on wheels, provided by a private firm on contract to the council, but she prefers the food my sister and I cook, so we stock up the freezer for them. Dad defrosts something for lunch and cooks it in the microwave, but he sometimes falls asleep and forgets about tea. Then the Share the Care lady does it.

'Mum gets the full Attendance Allowance, and all of it goes on paying for the carers who come in and look after her. Which is how it should be.

'At first they were a bit overwhelmed at having so many different people coming round all the time – especially my Dad. But they've got used to it now. Mum has got very fond of her regular personal care ladies – in fact I think she prefers them looking after her to me and my sister. They're very gentle, and they know just what they're doing. The lady who comes in the morning to wash her gives her a massage with scented oil. She doesn't have to do it – she just does it because she knows Mum likes it. She's so kind. In fact, they've all been so kind.'

Who will be responsible for your relative?

The worker in the social services department who is mainly responsible for looking after your relative's needs may be called her **key worker**. For most people who have help at home the key worker is the home care organiser. The key worker should inform the local social services team if they become worried about your relative's condition and thinks she needs to be reassessed. However, if you feel your relative's condition has deteriorated and she should be reassessed, you can ask for this to be done. You don't have to wait for the key worker to ask for a reassessment.

If your relative's needs are complicated, and a lot of different people are involved in looking after her, then someone may be appointed to be her **care manager** (in some areas they may be called **care co-ordinator** or

care organiser or **link worker**). This person is responsible for liaising with all the different people who provide care for your relative, and making sure they all work together. They may also contact the local clinic or surgery and ask the district nurse, health visitor or community psychiatric nurse to call on your relative, if they are worried about her health. (See pp 38–41 for an explanation of the roles of the different health care workers.)

Making interim arrangements

If your relative really wants to stay at home but feels she cannot cope on her own immediately, you may have to make temporary arrangements for the first few weeks.

Convalescent care in a care home

If your relative's needs are assessed by social services, as described on pages 19–21, she may be offered convalescent care in a residential or nursing home for two or three weeks as part of a 'care package'. If she has savings of £8,000 or less, the local authority should contribute towards the cost of care. The value of your relative's home will not be counted as part of her savings if the admission to a care home is to be temporary (see pp 82–83 for more about paying for care in a residential or nursing home).

If your relative is not offered convalescent care of this sort and you feel she needs it, you can ask the local authority to provide it. If this is still refused, you could consider whether either you or your relative could afford to pay for care yourselves. A couple of weeks being looked after in a care home could make all the difference to your relative's ability to manage on her own in the long term, with the help of whatever support services you have arranged. Trying to manage on her own too soon could even mean that the arrangements break down and your relative ends up feeling that she cannot manage at home and going into a residential or nursing home permanently.

If your relative does spend a couple of weeks convalescing in a care home, you may still find that you need to spend a week or so with her when she comes out, as the transition from having everything done for her to managing alone may be too abrupt. Or you may feel that an overnight stay with her when she comes out, with very frequent visits for the next couple of weeks, is a better way to ease the transition.

Other options for temporary care

If the local authority do not offer convalescent care, and you feel you can't afford to pay for it yourselves, or your relative hates the idea of going into a care home even temporarily, you will need to consider other short-term options. These could include:

▶ Your relative comes to stay with you (or another family member) for a few weeks.

▶ You (or another family member) stay with her for a few weeks.

▶ You and another family member (or members) take it in turns to look after her.

▶ You employ someone from a private agency to live in and look after her for a few weeks. The United Kingdom Home Care Association (address on p 119) can give you information about organisations that provide home care in your area. Another agency worth approaching is Care Alternatives (address on p 109).

Reassessing the situation

Whatever arrangements you make, you cannot be sure that things will work out exactly as you have planned. You and another family member may arrange to look after your relative alternative weeks for four weeks in all. Both you and your relative may feel sure she will be able to manage alone after this. But she may not recover as quickly as you all expected, or her condition could get worse rather than better. You would then have to rethink the situation completely. Making a long-term decision about your relative's future is the subject of Chapter 5.

CHECKLIST OF SUPPORT SERVICES AT HOME	
Help with your daily routine	*Whom to contact*
Help with housework, shopping, cleaning	*Social services, voluntary organisation or private agency*
Help with getting up, getting washed and dressed, going to the toilet, eating, getting undressed, going to bed	*Social services or voluntary care attendant scheme (eg Crossroads) or private agency (eg Care Alternatives)*

Help with incontinence or incontinence supplies (pads, pants, bedding)	District nurse or continence adviser (ask the GP)
Help with nursing, bathing, toileting, lifting	District nurse (ask the GP) or private nursing agency
Laundry service	Social services (many areas no longer offer this service) or private laundry service (look in the Yellow Pages)

Help with meals	*Whom to contact*
Meals on wheels	Social services or voluntary organisations (eg Age Concern or WRVS – Women's Royal Voluntary Service)
Luncheon club	Social services, local community group, church or voluntary group

Help with medical problems	*Whom to contact*
Advice about most general health problems	Your relative's GP, who may refer her to someone else
Nursing care at home, eg injections, changing dressings, etc	District nurse (ask the GP) or private nursing agency
Advice about lifting or turning someone heavy	District nurse or physiotherapist (ask the GP)
Advice on mobility and exercise	Physiotherapist (ask the GP)
Foot care, help with nail cutting	NHS chiropodist (ask the GP or district nurse) or private chiropodist

Help with aids, equipment and home adaptations	*Whom to contact*
Advice on equipment to help with everyday living, eg washing, cooking, using the toilet	Occupational therapist (social services department or hospital) or disability living centre (contact the Disability Living Centres Council)
Equipment for bedroom (rails, hoist, etc)	District nurse or occupational therapist (social services)
Mobility aids, eg wheelchair, walking sticks, walking frames	GP, physiotherapist or hospital (ask the GP)

Short-term hire of equipment	*British Red Cross (ask at the local branch), local Age Concern group, the WRVS or other organisations*
Adaptations to make your home more suitable for a disabled person	*Occupational therapist (social services department), housing or environmental health department, or voluntary organisation (eg Care and Repair)*

Help with getting about	***Whom to contact***
Help with transport	*Dial-a-ride or other voluntary organisation, social services or private taxi*
Transport to and from voluntary luncheon club, day centre, etc	*Social services or community group*
Transport to shops	*Community or voluntary group, Good Neighbour scheme (ask at social services). Some large stores run a bus service*
Advice about getting a specially adapted car	*Motability, Department of Social Security*
Orange parking badge	*Social services*
Disabled Person's Railcard	*Local railway station*

Social activities	***Whom to contact***
Day centre, luncheon or social club	*Social services, voluntary organisation (eg local Age Concern or Alzheimer's Disease Society group) or community centre*
Holidays	*Social services or voluntary group (eg Carers National Association), Holiday Care Service*

A break for the carer (respite care)	***Whom to contact***
Someone to sit with your relative while you go out for a few hours	*Social services, voluntary organisation (eg Crossroads or Share the Care) or private agency (eg Care Alternatives)*
Day care for your relative in a special centre; may include lunch, social activities, use of bathing facilities, chiropody, hairdressing, etc	*Social services, hospital or voluntary organisation (eg Age Concern, Help the Aged or Alzheimer's Disease Society)*

| Short-term care away from home, from a day to a fortnight. Could be in a hospital, residential or nursing home, or even with another family | Social services, hospital, private or voluntary residential or nursing home |

FOR MORE INFORMATION

▶ Age Concern England Factsheet 6 *Finding help at home.*

▶ Age Concern England Briefing Paper *Hospital Discharge Procedures*, available free from the Information and Policy Department, Age Concern England (address on p 121).

▶ *Caring at Home: A handbook for people looking after someone at home* by Nancy Kohner, published by NEC and the King's Fund (Tel: 0223 316644).

▶ *Who Cares Now? Caring for an older person* by Nancy Kohner and Penny Mares, published by BBC Education.

▶ *The Community Care Handbook: The new system explained* by Barbara Meredith, published by ACE Books (details on p 122).

Adapting the home

It is worth taking a good look at your relative's home and seeing if there are any changes which could make it safer or more convenient to live in.

Apart from general repairs and improvements, such as installing damp-proofing and insulation, you could make alterations to make the house more suited to the needs of an older or disabled person by adding:

▶ ramps leading up to doors with steps;

▶ a stronger stair rail;

▶ grab-rails by doors, and in the bathroom and toilet;

▶ wider doorways, to allow for a wheelchair;

▶ extra heating, or more convenient heating;

▶ a downstairs toilet and/or bathroom;

▶ a walk-in shower;

▶ a stair lift or other internal lift.

You could also consider a **home alarm system**. Find out whether there is a council-run scheme in your area, or you could consider buying an alarm for your relative. Most alarms are simple pendants that can be worn round the neck, and they work through the telephone system. It means that if your relative does have a fall, she can call for help. A number of organisations, such as Help the Aged or Age Concern ComCare Ltd, run community alarm schemes.

For further suggestions about simple things you can do to make the home safer, see pages 61–62.

Getting advice

If your relative has a disability, the best person to advise about any alterations to her home is an **occupational therapist (OT)**. OTs are trained to look at how people with disabilities can manage everyday tasks, such as getting about, washing, using the toilet, cooking, preparing drinks, eating, etc, and to suggest ways these could be made easier. OTs will advise about 'aids' – gadgets or equipment such as special taps for people who have difficulty with normal ones, or magnifiers for partially sighted people – as well as about actual alterations to the home. OTs can be based either in a hospital or in the social services department of your local council.

You may find there is a long wait for this service. In some areas, agencies called **Care and Repair** or **Staying Put** have been set up specially to advise older people and people with disabilities about repairing and adapting their homes. To find out whether there is a branch near where your relative lives, look in the telephone directory, ask the local housing department, or contact Care and Repair (address on p 109).

Grants from the council

Your relative may be able to get a grant from the local council towards the cost of certain improvements and alterations. This will depend on what income and savings she has, and on whether the council has the money.

There are two kinds of grants: **mandatory** grants are grants the council has to pay if the work qualifies and a person's income and savings are low. With **discretionary** grants it is up to the council to decide whether to give them or not. Nowadays, most councils do not have money available for discretionary grants, but it is still worth checking the situation locally.

Renovation grants are mandatory grants, paid for essential repairs or to provide essential services such as an indoor toilet or a bath or shower with hot and cold water.

Minor works grants are discretionary grants, available for smaller repairs and alterations. You may also get a minor works grant for alterations to enable a person aged 60 or over to move into a carer's home, such as installing a downstairs toilet. If the work costs more than the amount of the grant (a maximum of £1,080 in 1993), you will have to make up the difference yourself.

Grants are also available to provide facilities for a disabled person. These are called **disabled facilities grants**. They may be mandatory if an occupational therapist says that the facilities are essential.

You should *never* start the work before getting the council's approval to go ahead, or you will automatically be disqualified from receiving a grant.

Who qualifies?

Whether or not your relative will get a **renovation grant** depends mainly on her income and savings.

Savings of up to £5,000 are ignored. For savings above £5,000, an extra £1 is added to your relative's weekly income figure for every £250 of savings. If her income is above the limit for a grant, she may still be able to get a partial grant – ask the local council to work it out.

The income and savings limits for **disabled facilities grants** are largely the same as for renovation grants. Applicants for **minor works grants** must receive Income Support, Housing Benefit, Council Tax Benefit or Family Credit.

Can tenants apply for a grant?

Some tenants can apply for a disabled facilities grant, but they need their landlord's permission. Private tenants cannot usually apply for a renovation grant, but the landlord may be able to get one. If the house is in bad repair, tenants should contact the local council's environmental health department. They have the power to make the landlord do essential repairs. Housing association tenants should contact their local or regional office. Council tenants may be able to get a disabled facilities grant but not a renovation grant or a minor works grant.

Finding out about grants

The council's **renovation grants section** can advise you or your relative about grants and work out whether you qualify. If your relative is a tenant, they can advise her landlord about applying. Ring the council and ask for the department which deals with renovation grants, which is usually the environmental health or housing department.

If your relative cannot get a grant

Your relative may find that she cannot get a grant, either because she does not qualify for one or because the council has no money available. If she owns her own home, she could consider the possibility of raising some money on the value of the property, as explained in the publications listed below.

FOR MORE INFORMATION

▶ Age Concern England Factsheet 13 *Older home owners – financial help with repairs.*

▶ Age Concern England Factsheet 33 *Feeling safer at home and outside.*

▶ Age Concern England Factsheet 12 *Raising income or capital from your home.*

▶ *An Owner's Guide: Your Home in Retirement,* published by ACE Books (details on p 122).

▶ *Using Your Home as Capital,* published annually by ACE Books (details on p 123).

▶ **The Disabled Living Centres Council** (address on p 112) can advise you about special equipment and adaptations to the home to make life easier and safer for a disabled person. They can also give you a list of disabled living centres, where you can go and see the items of equipment that are available.

3 Whom to contact

If you are already feeling anxious and under pressure, nothing is more likely to reduce you to complete desperation than not knowing whom to contact about your relative – making one phone call only to be referred somewhere else, phoning the new number and perhaps being referred on yet again. This chapter aims to help you contact the right person, and to unravel the overlapping roles and responsibilities of the many different people who may be involved with the care of your relative.

The two key places where you may find help with arranging care for your relative are the **GP's surgery** *and the* **social services department**. *The GP is responsible for your relative's medical treatment. He or she is the person who will arrange the hospital and community-based health care. The social services department is responsible for organising services such as home care/home help and meals on wheels. Another key person is the* **district nurse**. *The GP or someone from social services may ask the district nurse to call if your relative needs nursing at home.*

❝By now Mum was feeling very anxious and depressed. She didn't know who to turn to.❞

When Penny's father was diagnosed as having leukaemia he was told he had only a 20 per cent chance of surviving chemotherapy. The consultant haematologist at the hospital seemed brusque and unapproachable. It was hard to get information about the treatment, and how to cope with the after-effects of chemotherapy.

'When the chemotherapy was finished, he was transferred to a general ward, and there wasn't really anybody who could answer our questions or tell us what was happening. I felt the staff weren't really trained to cope with the physical and emotional aspects of caring for someone with cancer, as they would be in a special cancer hospital or cancer unit.

'By now Mum was feeling very anxious and depressed. She didn't know who to turn to. Dad was withdrawn, and, as the chemotherapy went on, became increasingly rambling and confused.

'Then Mum heard about CancerLink, the cancer charity. They gave her a lot of information, and suggested questions she could ask the consultant. They also put her in touch with the local Leukaemia Care Society, who had informative leaflets, and a whole network of local contacts Mum could turn to.

'They also told her about the Macmillan nurses. But when she asked whether she could get counselling, the consultant was opposed to it. I think he didn't really understand what counselling was about. He thought it was for people who were preparing to die.'

Fortunately, they had a sympathetic GP, who arranged for Penny's father to be seen by a psychogeriatrician.

'He confirmed that Dad's confusion was due to the chemotherapy. This seemed to change the consultant's attitude. Mum did get to see the Macmillan nurse counsellor, and found her very helpful.

'The nurse put Mum in touch with the Carers National Association, who helped them to apply for Attendance Allowance. She also put them on to the local hospice, where Dad was able to attend the day centre and have regular physiotherapy. This was a lifeline for Mum.'

Who's who in social services

The key department of your local council for people needing care is the social services department. Under the new NHS and Community Care Act 1990, the social services department must assess what care a person needs, and co-ordinate all the different care services if they decide to offer help. The person from social services who is responsible for your relative should liaise with the GP, the district nurse, and if necessary the hospital.

UNDERSTANDING YOUR LOCAL COUNCIL

You may find yourself having to deal with various departments of the council, especially social services and housing. Local councils (also called local authorities) are organised differently according to where you live.

Big cities are usually **metropolitan boroughs** (or **metropolitan districts**) such as Tameside or Rotherham. All the services in the city come under the control of the borough (or district) council. London is divided into a number of **London boroughs** such as Haringey or Sutton, which are responsible for all the services in that area.

In other areas, the local council covers a whole **county** such as Devon or Lincolnshire. The county is usually divided into **districts**. The county is responsible for some services, such as social services, and the district for others, such as housing. This can be very confusing. If you are not sure, look in your telephone directory.

How social services departments are organised

All social services departments are organised differently, and the jobs people do have different names in different parts of the country. What is more, many social services departments have just gone through a big reorganisation to fit in with the new community care rules, so they may still be unsure of how the new system will work in practice. All this can make things difficult for people wanting help or information.

Most social services departments have a head office and a number of areas or districts. Within each district there may be two or three smaller teams covering local communities. (These are called **neighbourhood** or **community** or **locality** or **patch** or **area** teams.) It will usually be the local team which arranges care services for your relative.

Local teams

Each local team will have a **team leader** or **service manager** and a number of **social workers**. The social workers may be specialists, who specialise in working with children, people with disabilities, elderly people, people with learning disabilities, etc. Or they may be 'generic' social workers: that means that they do not specialise, but look after all kinds of people. Social workers help people with personal and financial problems, arrange services for them, and give information about other sources of help.

In addition, the local team will probably include some staff who are not fully qualified social workers, but who help them and take on some of the more straightforward cases. These could be called **welfare assistants** or **support workers** or **unqualified social workers** or **community care workers** or a similar name.

The home care organiser

Home care organisers (sometimes called **domestic services organisers**) may be attached to local teams. They are responsible for organising **home care workers** or **home care assistants**. These used to be called home helps, and their job was to come into people's homes and help with basic housework and shopping. Some councils still call them home helps. Sometimes they help with personal tasks such as helping someone get washed and dressed. In this case, they may be called **personal care assistants** or **personal care aides**.

Other services

In some places, the local teams are also responsible for day care centres, meals on wheels, and residential and nursing homes. But in some places these services are organised centrally. It can be quite hard to find out who is responsible for what service.

The occupational therapist

Another important member of the team is the **occupational therapist**. Their job is to come into the home and advise about aids and adaptations which can make living at home safer and easier for an elderly or disabled person. They will advise people about possible changes to their homes, such as fitting grab-rails, buying beds or special chairs, or making changes to toilet or washing facilities. They can also give advice about gadgets such as special cups and cutlery for people with arthritis, lightweight teapots, dustpans and brushes with long handles, and many other things to make life easier.

If you don't know whom to contact

Things are done differently in different parts of the country, so don't worry if you don't understand exactly how the local council is organised. The important thing is to be able to contact the right person to get the care your relative needs. If you seem to be getting nowhere, the local Age Concern group or carers' group may be able to advise you.

It is a good idea to try and find out if your relative has a care manager or key worker (see p 24) and make a note of his or her name and phone number. In an emergency, if you do not know whom to contact, ring up and ask for the **duty officer**. There should be a duty officer available at any time of day or night, and they will advise you what to do, or pass your details on to the right person. If you cannot get hold of anyone who can help you, dial 999 and ask for the police.

NOTE Some people get confused between social services and social security. **Social services** is a department of the local council which is responsible for looking after people in the community who need help, for example children, elderly people, people with disabilities, and people with mental health problems.

Social security is a department of the Government which is responsible for people's welfare and for payment of pensions, benefits, etc. The section that deals with benefits is now called the **Benefits Agency**.

Who's who in the health service

Many older people who need care and help at home have health problems and medical needs as well. The 1990 NHS and Community Care Act is supposed to make it easier for the health services and social services to work together.

The National Health Service provides both community-based and hospital-based health services.

Community-based health services

When someone is ill, their first contact with the health service is usually at the GP's surgery or the local clinic or health centre. Apart from the GP, you may also be able to be put in touch with a **practice nurse**, a **health visitor**, a **district nurse** or a **community psychiatric nurse**.

The GP is the key person who can put patients in touch with all the other health services. She or he may ask the district nurse, health visitor or community psychiatric nurse to call on patients who need care in their own homes. The GP may also decide to refer them to the local social services department or to a hospital consultant if they need specialist medical care. Some GPs have their own budgets, with which they buy a range of services for their patients; they are called GP fundholders.

Social workers should liaise with the community-based health services, to make sure people get all the help they need.

If someone needs hospital treatment they are usually referred to a consultant by their GP. But in an emergency you can dial 999 for an ambulance, or just go along to the casualty department.

NOTE You might like to have the name and phone number of your relative's GP, and of the district nurse, if your relative wishes this.

Professional	What they do
General practitioner (GP)	*Your family doctor, who can put patients in touch with a range of health services*
District nurse	*Helps with practical nursing, eg bathing, lifting, turning, toileting, giving injections, changing dressings, etc. Can show you how to do these where appropriate*
Health visitor	*Visits families, usually with young children; sometimes visits elderly people and advises about other services*
Community psychiatric nurse (CPN)	*Visits and advises people with mental health problems and their carers*
Link worker	*Works with people whose mother tongue is not English; sometimes acts as an advocate (someone who speaks on behalf of a person as if they were speaking for that person)*
Interpreter	*Helps people whose mother tongue is not English*
Continence adviser	*Offers advice, help and information about incontinence, including practical aids (pads, pants, etc). Ask the district nurse or GP to ask them to call*
Chiropodist	*Provides free NHS chiropody for older people, especially those with mobility problems (ask the GP or district nurse)*
Dentist	*Some dentists will visit at home (ask your local dentist or contact the Family Health Services Authority)*
Optician	*Some opticians make home visits (ask your local optician or contact the Family Health Services Authority)*

Hospital-based health services

Doctors

A patient who comes into hospital is put under the care of a **consultant**, who is a specialist doctor. These are some hospital specialists you may come across:

Cardiologist Specialist in heart disease.

Geriatrician Specialises in treating older people.

Neurologist Treats diseases of the brain and nervous system.

Oncologist Cancer specialist.

Ophthalmologist Specialises in eye problems.

Orthopaedic surgeon Treats injuries and diseases of the bones by surgery.

Psychiatrist Treats people with mental health problems.

Psychogeriatrician Specialises in mental illnesses in older people, for example dementia.

Rheumatologist Specialises in diseases of muscles and joints, for example rheumatism and arthritis.

Urologist Treats disorders of the bladder and urinary tract, including prostate problems.

Under the consultant are a number of other doctors who are less experienced, but still fully qualified. These may be **senior registrars** or **registrars**, or they may be **junior doctors** or **house officers**. They are usually responsible for the day-to-day treatment of patients.

Nurses

While the doctors decide on medical treatment, such as prescribing drugs and performing surgery, the nurses decide on nursing care and provide care and support for the patient. So nurses and doctors work together as a team.

The nurse with overall responsibility for the running of the ward is the **sister** or **charge nurse** or **ward manager**. Below the sister is the **staff nurse**, who will be a State Registered Nurse or Registered Nurse, and State Enrolled Nurses. There may also be student nurses, nursing auxiliaries, nursing assistants, and health care support workers, none of whom are fully qualified nurses.

Some nurses are hospital-based, but can also visit at home to provide specialist care, for example:

Diabetic liaison nurse For diabetics requiring special care.

Stoma care nurse For patients who have had a colostomy.

Mastectomy counsellor or **breast care nurse** For women who need surgery for breast cancer.

Macmillan nurse For cancer patients and their families.

Other hospital-based professionals who sometimes visit at home include:

Occupational therapist Helps patients manage everyday tasks, and advises on any equipment for the home that may be needed.

Speech therapist Shows people with speech difficulties how to speak, sometimes working with stroke patients.

Physiotherapist Helps people who have pain or difficulty in moving, using exercises, massage, manipulation, ultrasound, and other physical treatments.

Dietician Draws up special diets for patients to help them control their illness, and advises patients accordingly.

Dealing with 'the system'

Sometimes finding the right help is not easy, and you may feel frustrated and angry at all the delays and red tape. These hints may help you in dealing with social services staff or health care staff:

Remember, you are important As a caring relative or friend you are important to your relative's well-being. In fact your support and love may be more important to her than all the other services put together.

Be well prepared Before you talk to social services or health care staff, make a list of all the points you want to mention. Then tick them off as you go along. Make a note of what they say.

Be polite but firm You may find it helps to have someone with you for moral support when you meet with social services or health care staff.

See the other person's point of view If you are feeling upset or angry it can be hard to listen properly to what the other person is saying. Remember that they are only human too. It may help if you can show you are sympathetic to their position. ('I know you're under a lot of pressure . . .' 'I really appreciate what you've done so far . . .' 'I know you want the best for my mother/father/uncle/aunt but . . .')

Keep names and phone numbers Make a list of the names and phone numbers of all the people you deal with, and note down what they do. You may want to put a star against the names of people who were particularly helpful.

Keep a record of dates Record the date when you spoke to someone, and make a note of when they said something would happen. Then you can chase them up if it doesn't materialise.

Don't be afraid to complain If you are not happy with the way you are treated, don't be afraid to complain. All social services departments have a complaints procedure, which they are obliged to tell clients about. Just ring up the main number and say you want to make a complaint. They will tell you whom to contact. Usually, the person to contact will be the social services team leader for the area where your relative lives. If you want to complain about health services, it is best to contact the Community Health Council for further advice on how to do this.

WHERE TO GO FOR INFORMATION AND ADVICE

Help needed	Where to go
Information about your relative's illness or disability	*There may be a voluntary group or charity which can give advice and information (see address list on pp 107–120)*
Information about welfare benefits	*The Citizens Advice Bureau, local Benefits Agency (social security) office or local advice centre, or phone the Benefits Agency Freeline 0800 666 555*
Information about what services are available for your relative	*The social services department of the area where your relative lives (see checklist of support services on pp 26–29) or the GP*
Advice and information about adapting your relative's home	*The occupational therapist at the social services department or Care and Repair (see p 109) or the renovation grants section of your relative's local council*

Advice about most general health problems	*The GP*
Nursing care or advice about mobility, lifting or turning someone heavy	*District nurse*
Advice about incontinence	*Continence adviser*
Information about making a Will or other legal matters	*Citizens Advice Bureau, law centre or solicitor (see pp 97–98)*
Someone to talk to about your own problems	*Contact your own GP, who may refer you to the community psychiatric nurse or to a counsellor or to MIND (address on p 114)*
Support in bereavement	*CRUSE, the Compassionate Friends or Lesbian and Gay Bereavement Project (see pp 110, 111 and 114 for addresses). Hospitals, hospices and churches may also offer support*
Contact with other carers	*Ask the social worker if there is a carers' group, or contact the local Council for Voluntary Service or the Carers National Association (address on p 109)*
If you feel desperate	*Contact the Samaritans. Their number will be in your local telephone directory*

NOTE In an emergency, if you don't know who to contact or can't get hold of them, dial 999 and ask for an ambulance if it is a health emergency, or the police for any other emergency.

4 Common health crises in older people

This section looks at some of the health problems that are most common in older people which may require emergency treatment and may create a crisis situation for the family. We look at dementia (including Alzheimer's disease), heart attack, stroke, cancer, and injury as a result of a fall. Some of the medical terms and treatments you may come across are explained.

Although dementia develops gradually over a number of years, it is included here because it is so often a crisis – an accident at home, a sudden illness, or the person suddenly wandering away and getting lost – which alerts the family to the need to take action. Cancer, too, develops gradually, but there may be points in the course of the disease when a crisis occurs, for example when it is first diagnosed and immediate treatment is necessary, or in the final stages.

For more detailed information, you are advised to go to one of the organisations or charities which specialise in that particular illness. These are listed at the end of each section.

❝We were horrified to realise the danger he'd been in.❞

Roy realised his father was getting a bit absent-minded and strange in his ways, but he didn't think anything of it until one night he was woken up by a knock on the door. It was the police. They had Roy's father in the back of the car. He was in his pyjamas and dressing gown.

'They'd picked Dad up wandering along the edge of the motorway. He said he'd lost his way. We were horrified to realise the danger he'd been in.

'We'd always thought he was quite happy living on his own. My wife or I dropped by every day. And he had good neighbours, who kept an eye on him after my mother died. They did tell us that he would occasionally knock on their door late at night, but they always made him a cup of tea and sent him home. This time they were away, and we think he must have set out to try and find us. Thank goodness the police picked him up before anything happened.

'We realised he wouldn't be able to live on his own any longer, but we really had no idea what to do. We put him to bed in our room and my wife and I bedded down on the sofa-bed downstairs. We didn't get much sleep. We spent the whole night talking about what to do.

'The police told us to contact social services, and they sent somebody round next day. They said it would be best if he went into a residential home. Dad was very upset at the idea. He said we were locking him away. But after he'd been to see the home he perked up a bit. He likes company, and there were plenty of people to talk to. There's even someone on duty at night if he feels like taking a midnight wander.'

Dementia

What is it?

The dementias are a group of diseases in which the brain progressively degenerates. **Alzheimer's disease** is a common cause; another is **multi-infarct dementia**. It is estimated that one in five people over the age of 80 suffer from dementia.

People with dementia gradually lose their mental faculties and become confused. They tend to forget things that have happened quite recently, but may seem to have a clear memory of things that happened a long time ago. Their personality may also change. They may do or say strange and inappropriate things. They may wander about restlessly, especially at night. They may become angry and aggressive towards the person who cares for them, or they may become childlike and dependent. They may forget where they have put things, and accuse others of stealing them. They may forget to eat or to wash themselves, and they may put themselves and others at risk, for example by turning on the gas and forgetting to light it. All this can be very difficult and stressful for the carer, especially if the person is someone they have loved for many years.

A few early onset (before 60 years old) cases of Alzheimer's disease are thought to have a genetic cause (ie the tendency runs in families), but in the vast majority of cases the cause is unknown, despite continuing research efforts. Several factors are thought to predispose people to develop multi-infarct dementia, including smoking, overuse of alcohol, uncorrected high blood pressure and poorly controlled diabetes.

Not all confusion in older people is due to dementia. If your relative suddenly becomes confused or seems to lose her memory, it is important for her to see a doctor, as the confusion could be due to a physical illness or medicines she is taking.

What is the outlook?

Alzheimer's disease and multi-infarct dementia are progressive and ultimately fatal illnesses. That means that sufferers get gradually worse, and eventually die. How long someone will live depends a lot on their general health, and the age at which they develop the disease. Your GP or the hospital consultant are the best people to talk to about how the disease will affect your relative.

Some people with dementia manage to live in their own homes for quite a long time, with support from their family, social services and community health teams. After a while, however, it may be too risky for them to live on their own. It often happens that a sudden crisis, such as an illness or an accident, makes us aware that they can no longer cope alone.

At this point, a decision has to be made whether they will live with a family member or go into a residential or nursing home (see pp 75–83).

Caring for someone with dementia

Caring for someone with dementia can be very stressful; it is not something that everybody can take on. If you decide this is the right option for you, then you will find it helpful to have as much information as possible about your relative's condition (see p 15). You should also find out what support you can get through social services (see pp 26–29).

How you can help your relative

▶ Help your relative's memory by having familiar objects and photographs around. Encourage her to keep a diary and to write things down. Keep a calendar and clock on view, and refer to them when you talk. Establish a regular routine.

▶ Make sure that your relative's physical health is looked after, and that eyesight and hearing problems are diagnosed and dealt with, as these can add to confusion.

▶ Encourage self-esteem and independence. Treat your relative as an adult, help her to be clean and tidy, and encourage her to do as much as she can for herself, or to do simple tasks around the house.

▶ Avoid clashes, confrontations and arguments. It is better to change the subject, or distract her, than to get into a head-on row. But don't go along with muddled thinking or delusions. Just point out tactfully that you see things differently.

▶ Be very careful about safety in the home, especially where cooking, fires and gas are concerned. A person with dementia may forget that they have turned an appliance on, or turn on the gas and forget to light it.

Taking good care of yourself

Caring for a person with dementia is both physically tiring and emotionally stressful. Your relative may often keep you awake at night, or she may suddenly turn on you for no apparent reason, or she may forget who you are. As a carer, you will need plenty of help and support.

These DOs and DON'Ts may help:

Do look after your own health. See your own GP about health problems, and don't be afraid to mention psychological or emotional problems.

Do find out about respite care, so that you can have a break from time to time (see pp 28–29).

Do make contact with other carers. They could be your lifeline. You can find out about carers' groups in your area through the social services department, the local Age Concern group, the Carers National Association or the Alzheimer's Disease Society (addresses on pp 109 and 107).

Don't be afraid to ask for the help you need, from social services, your doctor or your family.

Don't think you have to go on caring forever. As your relative's dementia progresses, you may feel that residential or nursing home care is the only solution.

Don't feel guilty about it if you do make this decision.

FOR MORE INFORMATION

▶ **The Alzheimer's Disease Society** (address on p 107) produces a number of useful books and leaflets. They will also put you in touch with other people in your area, so that you can share problems and information.

▶ *The 36-Hour Day* by Nancy L Mace and Peter V Rabins MD with Beverly A Castleton, Evelyn McEwen and Barbara Meredith, published jointly by ACE Books and Headway, is a comprehensive and informative guide to caring for someone with dementia.

Heart attack

What is it?

A heart attack happens when the blood supply to part of the heart is suddenly blocked by a blood clot. It is more likely to happen if the **arteries** (the blood vessels which take blood to the body) are unhealthily clogged with a fatty substance called **atheroma.** Atheroma restricts the free circulation of the blood and encourages blood clots to form. A blood clot which blocks the artery where it is formed is called a **thrombus**, while one which is carried in the bloodstream from a different part of the body is called an **embolus**. Both are very dangerous.

The arteries which carry blood to the heart are called **coronary arteries**. If a thrombus forms in one of these, it is called a **coronary thrombosis**, which is another name for a heart attack.

If the arteries are badly clogged up with atheroma, a severe chest pain called **angina** is sometimes felt. This is a warning that a heart attack could happen, so if this occurs you should see the doctor at once. However, some heart attacks happen without any warning.

In a heart attack, the part of the heart where the blood has been cut off is damaged. The pain can be very intense, affecting not just the chest but sometimes the neck, jaw and inner arm as well. Some older people may have little or no pain. They may instead become faint, fall, have an attack of vomiting or become confused.

Smoking, high blood pressure, diabetes or unusually high levels of fat (**cholesterol**) in the blood are all factors which contribute to a build-up of atheroma and make a heart attack more likely.

MINA

❜ Suddenly he just crumpled up with this terrible pain in his chest. ❜

'It came as such a shock when my husband had a heart attack. He was only 62, and he'd always seemed so fit and well, even if he did smoke a little bit more than he ought. He'd been complaining about pains in his chest a few days before, but I didn't think anything of it. I thought it was indigestion. Then suddenly he just crumpled up with this terrible pain in his chest. I phoned the ambulance, and fortunately they were pretty quick.

'They got him into hospital, and wired him up to all sorts of hi-tech machines. He looked so pitiful lying there with wires stuck all over him. What amazed me was the way they had him out of bed and walking about after a few days. I thought it was a bit cruel, but apparently that's what they do nowadays.

'At first, I was just relieved he was still alive. And with all the fuss and attention he was getting, we didn't really think about the future. Then they moved him off the special cardiac ward on to the general ward. He was with a lot of old men – at least, they seemed old – and he started to get depressed and anxious. "I don't look as old as them do I, Mina?" he'd say. Of course I reassured him, but the truth was, my view of him had changed. I'd always thought of him as the strong one in our relationship. Now I was seeing the vulnerable side of him.

'When he came home, it was even harder. He would swing between being optimistic and full of plans, and being down in the dumps. The doctor told me I should encourage him to do things for himself, not wait on him hand and foot. He said it was important to build up his independence. But I felt so mean.

'The best thing was, the doctor also told him he had to stop smoking and start regular exercise. He recommended walking. We started going out into the countryside during the week, when there was no one else around. Sometimes we would set out early and stop for a pub lunch. We discovered lovely places we'd never known about. And it brought us close together again. We were like a young couple, walking through the fields holding hands.

'Yes, the heart attack has changed our lives, but it's had some good effects, too. Jay is not as caught up in his work as he used to be, he realises there are other things in life.'

What is the outlook?

The outlook for someone who has had a heart attack depends on how severe it was and how soon they can get to hospital. The first couple of hours are crucial, since this is when someone is most likely to die. If they survive for 24 hours, their chances of recovery are good. If there are no complications they may be sent home after about ten days, and will need to rest for another two or three months. Regular gentle exercise combined with drug treatment can help prevent another heart attack. Changes of lifestyle such as stopping smoking and taking a sensible diet may also help.

If one of the arteries is so badly narrowed that angina pains do not respond to treatment, surgery may be necessary. This is likely to take one of two forms. **Angioplasty** uses a hollow needle to insert a special small balloon into the artery. The balloon is then inflated, widening the artery, so that blood can flow more easily. **Coronary artery bypass surgery** involves grafting a vein from another part of the body to bypass the part of the artery which is blocked. A relatively new treatment is **thrombolysis**, which seeks to dissolve a clot before the heart muscle is irreversibly damaged. For best results this has to be done soon after the clot forms.

Caring for someone who has had a heart attack

A heart attack is a great shock, not just physically but also emotionally. It may leave someone feeling depressed and anxious for several months.

There are several ways in which you can help your relative if she has had a heart attack:

▶ Help her give up smoking. If you smoke yourself, and are living with someone who has had a heart attack, it will help them to give up if you stop smoking too – and it will also reduce your own risk of heart attack and cancer.

▶ Help her lose weight if she needs to. The doctor will tell her what her ideal weight should be, and will suggest a calorie-reducing diet if necessary. The main thing to cut down on is fats – especially animal fats found in red meat, butter, cheese, eggs and non-skimmed milk – as these can help cause the build-up of cholesterol in the blood which leads to atheroma.

▶ Help her to exercise regularly. It is important to stick to an exercise routine recommended by the doctor, and not to overdo it.

▶ Emphasise the positive; many people who have survived heart attacks have happy and productive lives afterwards.

Heart failure

Heart failure is different from a heart attack. It happens gradually, when the pumping mechanism in the heart is not working properly, because one or more of the heart valves is leaking, or because the heart muscle has been damaged, for example by a heart attack. When this happens, fluid can build up in the lungs, causing breathlessness, and in the ankles, causing them to swell. Heart failure is usually treated with tablets to remove the excess fluid and other medicines. Sometimes an operation is performed to repair or replace faulty heart valves.

▶ *Beating Heart Disease*, a leaflet from the Health Education Authority (address on p 113).

▶ **The British Heart Foundation** (address on p 108) has booklets about different kinds of heart disease, and recovery from a heart attack.

Stroke

What is it?

A stroke occurs when part of the brain dies because its blood supply is cut off. The patient can no longer perform the functions the dead bit of the brain used to control.

Every stroke has different effects, depending on which part of the brain is damaged, and how severely. The most common effect is partial paralysis and loss of feeling on one side of the body – the opposite side to the part of the brain which is damaged. Mental ability, speech, vision and even personality can be affected. A stroke is sometimes called a cerebrovascular accident.

Sometimes stroke signs appear but rapidly get better, often within a few hours. This happens when the brain's blood supply is briefly cut off but is then restored. This is called a **transient ischaemic attack** or **TIA**. People with TIAs should see the doctor, as prompt treatment can prevent a later complete stroke, with irreversible brain damage.

Strokes are commoner in people who have high blood pressure, heart disease or diabetes or who have recently had a TIA. Smoking, being overweight, taking little exercise and drinking too much alcohol all add to the risk. People aged over 75 are most at risk.

❛I knew I had to keep her busy and cheerful.❜

Emily's mother was fit and active until she had a stroke, which left her paralysed down one side and unable to use her right arm. She then came to live with Emily and her family. She stayed with them for the next 20 years.

'She had always been a very active woman, and I knew I had to keep her busy and cheerful. She would still knit and iron with one hand. If I was cooking something, I would pass her the spoon and say, "Stir this for me, Mum."

'I think the grandchildren kept her going. They behaved as though there was nothing different about her. We all tried to keep her cheerful and optimistic – I think that's very important. I was lucky to have a car, and we have a caravan by the seaside. If she was feeling miserable I'd say, "Would you like some fish and chips?" and we'd go off somewhere for a treat.'

Emily's mother has recently died, and Emily is left with a feeling of emptiness.

'We were tied for all those years she lived with us. I thought I would appreciate the freedom, but I find I miss her a lot. It's a strange feeling, suddenly having so much time on my hands.'

What is the outlook?

Most people who survive a stroke recover their abilities to some degree. Much depends on the age and health of the person, and on how severe the brain damage was. Determination and will power are important too.

A physiotherapist can advise about exercises to get a person moving again, and a speech therapist will help if speech has been affected. It is important to start exercising as soon as possible so that stiffness and loss of movement do not set in and become permanent.

Caring for someone who has had a stroke

If your relative has had a stroke, you can help by making sure she does the exercises recommended by the physiotherapist and encouraging a positive attitude. Help her to get out and about, and make sure she takes any medicines that have been prescribed which will reduce the risk of a second stroke.

FOR MORE INFORMATION

▶ **The Stroke Association** (address on p 119) has information about caring for a stroke patient, and they can tell you about local stroke clubs where you can get help and advice.

Cancer

What is it?

Cancer is a disease in which some cells in the body start to multiply uncontrollably, causing a lump called a **tumour**. Not all tumours are caused by cancer. Lumps in tissue may form for many other reasons. A cancerous tumour is called **malignant**; a non-cancerous tumour is called **benign**.

Cancer can happen anywhere in the body, but the most common sites are the lungs, bowel and prostate in men, and the breasts, lung, cervix, uterus and ovaries in women. Other common cancers are **leukaemia** (cancer of the blood and bone marrow) and **lymphoma** (cancer of the lymph glands in the neck, armpits and groin).

When a tumour grows to a certain size it begins to shed some of its cancerous cells. These are carried around the body in the bloodstream or the lymph system, and settle in other sites where they cause new cancers to grow. This process is called **metastasis**, and cancers formed in this way are called **secondary cancers**.

Some cancers are linked to chemical substances, such as asbestos, coaltar or cigarette smoke. In other cancers, particularly cancers of the reproductive organs, hormones are thought to play a part. Radiation is known to cause cancer. Even radiation from the sun – in other words, sunshine – can cause skin cancer. Some cancers are thought to be caused by a virus, others by constant irritation or a wound that does not heal.

New anti-cancer research is concentrating increasingly on how we can boost the body's own defence mechanisms, which protect us from cancer most of the time.

PEGGY

6 **They told us he had a tumour as big as a grapefruit on his left lung. I was devastated.** 9

Peggy's husband Bill went to the doctor with a slight irritating cough that had been bothering him for a while. The doctor sent him to the hospital for an X-ray, and within four days the family were told that he had lung cancer.

'They told us he had a tumour as big as a grapefruit on his left lung. I was devastated. Bill put his arm round me and said, "We've been together for 45 years, and we'll get through this." Really, it was him that gave me strength.

'We were referred to the hospital, and after that everything seemed to happen very quickly. They took away his whole lung and some of the surrounding tissues. He had the operation on his 70th birthday.

'They kept him in a couple of weeks, and when he was allowed home, the district nurse came in every day to change his dressing. It was a huge cut, but it healed very well. Gradually he picked up, and we carried on. He couldn't play golf any more because he couldn't swing the golf club, but he still went round the course with his friends, and he still went fishing. We went on holiday as usual in July.

'Then he started to get these pains across his shoulder. Our hearts sank when they told us he would have to go to Weston Park. That's a specialist cancer hospital. We thought it was the end of the road. But everyone was so kind and friendly. It was a lovely atmosphere – not like a hospital at all. Even now, I would never be afraid of going into that hospital.

'He could still drive, so they let him come every day for his radiotherapy. We even went abroad on holiday that year, though he had to rest every afternoon.

'Then it spread down to his liver and tummy. He was sick a lot, and I was often up all night with him. He began to lose more weight, and he was very poorly. But he never lost his inner strength. However ill he'd been in the night, if someone came to see him next day, he always had a smile for them.

'At the end, it all happened very quickly. One day, he was still able to walk down to the bottom of the garden. That night, he was very ill. They asked him if he would prefer to go into hospital, but he wanted to stay at home, though he did agree to go into the hospice. But in the end it wasn't necessary. They offered us other help, too. We could have had a night nurse, and a special cancer care Macmillan nurse. But he didn't live long enough. We had two doctors from the local practice and two nurses popping in and out all the time. They put a needle in his hand, and there was a little pump which gave him a constant supply of painkiller, so he didn't suffer. We were all with him – the whole family. The vicar came and said a service round his bed. It was all so peaceful, just the way he would have wanted it to be.

'Although I was terribly upset, I think it happened the best way. We had four wonderful years after his first operation. Every day was a bonus.'

What is the outlook?

Cancer is by no means the dreaded incurable disease it was ten years ago. But it is still the second main cause of death in Britain (after heart disease) simply because it is more likely to happen in older people. All cancers are different, and the doctor is the best person to advise you about the outlook for your relative. Older people who remember how cancer used to be may be unduly pessimistic. Many people who are diagnosed as having cancer will live to die of an unrelated cause.

Caring for someone with cancer

Even when you are told that your relative has not long to live, there is still much you can do to make her last weeks or months comfortable and happy:

- ▶ Offer her small frequent meals, and plenty of drinks.

- ▶ If her mouth is dry and sore, offer cool drinks. The doctor may be able to prescribe something that helps.

- ▶ Help prevent pressure sores by moving or turning her regularly. The district nurse will show you how to do this.

- ▶ Take care of her skin with moisturiser or body oils, but avoiding skin which has been damaged by radiotherapy. A gentle massage can be soothing and comforting.

- ▶ Give painkillers regularly, rather than waiting until pain is severe. The doctor or nurse will tell you how much to give.

- ▶ Help prevent constipation by adding a little roughage to the diet, such as a teaspoonful of bran, or fresh fruit and vegetables. People on strong painkillers will need laxatives.

- ▶ If incontinence is a problem, ask the GP or district nurse about supplies and advice. They can also tell you whether there is a laundry service in your area.

- ▶ A radio by the bed, or a television with remote control, can help while away sleepless hours.

- ▶ Show your love, by sitting with your relative and talking to her, or just holding her hand and letting her talk to you about her worries and fears.

Other sources of help

Macmillan nurses are nurses specially trained to look after cancer patients and their families. They give both practical advice and emotional support. Their knowledge and experience are much valued by the people they work with. You can contact a Macmillan nurse through your doctor or hospital, or through the Cancer Relief Macmillan Fund (see below).

Sometimes, when a person cannot get the nursing care they need at home, they may be offered a place in a hospice. This is a special hospital for terminally ill patients, where the staff are highly skilled in pain relief, and at dealing with the emotional side of terminal illness. Some hospices have an outreach team to treat people in their own homes; find out more about these from the Hospice Information Service (address on p 113).

▶ **Cancer Relief Macmillan Fund** (address on p 109) can give you information about how to contact a Macmillan nurse in your area.

▶ **Cancerlink** (address on p 109) gives support and information about cancer, and can put you in touch with people in your area who have experience of the disease. Their free booklet *Caring for the Very Sick Person at Home* is full of practical advice and suggestions.

▶ **BACUP** (British Association of Cancer United Patients – address on p 108) has a telephone Cancer Information Service (071-608 1661) and a free helpline for people outside London (0800 181 199). It offers free information leaflets about different types of cancer, and a one-to-one counselling service for people in London. Telephone 071-606 1785 for an appointment.

All these cancer charities work closely together.

Falls and fractures

Elderly people are particularly at risk of accidents and injuries at home – especially falls. It is estimated that almost a third of people aged over 70 will have at least one fall at home in a year. Usually falls just cause bruising and superficial cuts – though even these can cause problems for frail elderly people. But the greatest risk is of fractures. Older people are especially at risk of fractures of the forearm and fractures of the hip. Hip fractures are more serious, because they can affect a person's mobility, and thus their ability to go on living independently, even after the fracture has healed. Crush fractures of the vertebrae are a cause of severe back pain, disability and deformity.

Anyone can have a fall, but some people are more at risk than others. These include:

▶ people who are confused or mentally ill;

▶ blind or partially sighted people;

▶ people who have had a stroke;

▶ people with chronic arthritis, Parkinson's disease, or other illnesses which can affect posture and stability;

▶ people with poor co-ordination or reflexes;

► people who are taking certain medicines, especially those with a sedative effect or which lower the blood pressure;

► people who have been drinking alcohol;

► people with some sorts of heart disease;

► people who have had a previous fall.

Older women who fall are more at risk of fracturing a bone. This is because after the menopause women's bones may become more fragile through **osteoporosis**. Men can develop this too as they age, but much more slowly and less severely than women do.

RAY

❝When I got there, she was still sitting in the same chair where the ambulance people had left her, and she had wet herself.❞

Ray's mother lives on her own. Last winter, she fell on the front doorstep and banged her head. Fortunately someone saw her and called an ambulance and she was taken to hospital. They did a very thorough check, and gave her an X-ray. They couldn't find anything wrong with her, so they put her in an ambulance and sent her home.

'At about six o'clock that night, I got a phone call from mother. She sounded terrible, but she couldn't explain what was wrong. She said she couldn't make a cup of tea.

'Well, I live a hundred miles away, but I couldn't think of anyone to contact. So I jumped in my car and drove up. When I got there, she was still sitting in the same chair where the ambulance people had left her, and she had wet herself. She was terribly distressed and embarrassed, as she had never been incontinent before. I cleaned her up and made her a meal and a hot drink. Then I put her to bed.

'Fortunately next day she was feeling much better, and she could get out of bed and potter around. I knew I would have to go back to work, so I spent the morning making a few phone calls and I organised a rota of people who would call in and make sure she was all right.

'The accident really made me aware of how vulnerable old people are living on their own, and I tried to persuade her to move into a sheltered bungalow or flat, where there would be someone to pop in regularly and make sure she is all right. The trouble is, she has lived in her house for 30 years, and doesn't really want to move.

'So, as a compromise, I got someone from the council to come round
and check the house out for us, and I also got some leaflets from
ROSPA (the Royal Society for the Prevention of Accidents). Fortunately
I'm quite handy, so I've been able to make a few changes around the
house – I've put a grab-rail in by the front doorstep where she tripped
and I've put a stair rail in, too. I've persuaded her to have a fitted carpet
in the hall instead of a loose runner, and I've put an extra length of flex
on the standard lamp, so it will go around the wall instead of across the
floor.

'Now she's got her confidence back, she seems very cheerful. In fact,
I'm the one who's worried. Before I left, I made sure I got the phone
numbers of a few of her friends, her GP, the district nurse and the local
social services. Now all I can do is keep my fingers crossed it won't
happen again. But if it does, I'll be a bit better prepared.'

What happens after a fall

If your relative does not have to stay in hospital

Someone who has had a fall, and is feeling bruised and shaken, may
be taken to hospital for an X-ray, to make sure they have not fractured a
bone. If there is no fracture, they will probably be sent straight home. Or
if the GP is called, he or she may think there is no need for them to go to
hospital.

If your relative has had a fall, it is important that she is not left alone, or
sent home from hospital to an empty house. Even though she may seem
to be all right at first she will probably stiffen up, and find it hard to move.
She may find it hard to get to the toilet, or to make herself something to
eat or drink. Her confidence is also likely to have taken a knock, so she
may not want to get up and move about. Or she may try to move, but be
so stiff and shaky that she has another fall. For all these reasons, it is
important that there is someone to keep an eye on her.

If you cannot stay with your relative, it is important to make sure that
someone can at least pop in a couple of times a day to help her to the toi-

let if necessary, or make a meal or a drink for her. Sometimes it is hard to know whom to contact, especially if it is the evening or weekend – see pages 14–15 for some suggestions.

Your relative may be sent straight home from hospital even if she does have a fracture. If she has a simple fracture, the limb may be put in plaster and she may then be sent home, or she may be kept in overnight for observation. Accident and Emergency Units are used to treating injuries, but may not be aware of the other needs and problems of older people.

Under the NHS and Community Care Act 1990, hospital discharge procedures are supposed to prevent this happening, but it does sometimes happen that an elderly person is sent home from hospital without any arrangements for them to be cared for at home. Always make sure you know when your relative is being discharged, and that there will be someone there to keep an eye on her at least for a day or two.

If your relative has to stay in hospital

A serious or complicated fracture may call for a long stay in hospital. In older people, a fracture of the hip is most likely to cause complications, so a hip replacement is often recommended. This usually means about five weeks in hospital. If your relative is not able to move about and get some exercise during this time, her muscles may get so weak that she is no longer able to walk. For this reason, the hospital will try to get your relative up and moving as soon as possible. This usually means taking a few steps the day after the operation. Discharge arrangements should be made as soon as possible, especially if home adaptations such as ramps and grab-rails are needed.

Making the home safer

There are a lot of simple, straightforward things which can be done to make the home safer.

Home safety checklist

▶ Remove all loose mats and rugs. Nail carpets down if possible.

▶ Make sure stair carpets are properly fitted.

▶ Fit a strong rail at the side of the staircase. If your relative has had a stroke, and can only use one arm, fit a rail on each side.

▶ Use higher-wattage light bulbs in corridors and stairways.

▶ Do not use cupboards or shelves which are so high that you need to stand on a chair to reach them. Use them for storing things which are seldom used, or leave them empty.

▶ Install grab-rails by the bath or shower and toilet.

▶ Use non-slip mats in the bath or shower if it does not already have a special non-slip surface.

▶ Install grab-rails by the front and back steps, and by any internal steps.

▶ Tape trailing flexes around the edges of the wall. Try to avoid tucking them under carpets, as they can fray without anyone realising it, and cause fires.

▶ Use extra table-lamps or side-lamps to lighten dark corners. This can also mean that if the ceiling light bulb goes your relative will not have to change it herself or wait in the dark until help arrives. (But make sure flexes do not trail across the floor.)

▶ If glass doors are not made of safety glass, cover them with a shatterproof film (from DIY shops).

▶ Have gas appliances and flues checked regularly. If possible, use gas installations with a flame supervision device – this means the gas will be turned off automatically if it is not lit.

▶ Have electrical wiring checked by an electrician. Make sure that sockets and fuses are not overloaded.

▶ If there are open fires, make sure there is a fireguard, and that it is easy to use.

If you or your relative has a bit of money to spend, you could also consider getting **fitted carpets** which reduce the risk of tripping or slipping, as well as being easy to keep clean. A **microwave cooker** may be easier to use, and may cut down the risk of burns on hot pans, provided your relative is capable of understanding the instructions. It is also more economical for cooking or heating up small quantities of food.

▶ See pages 29–30 for further suggestions about ways to make the home safer and more convenient for an older or disabled person to live in.

▶ Age Concern England Briefing Paper *Hospital Discharge Procedures* is available free from the Information and Policy Department, Age Concern England (address on p 121).

▶ *Safety in Your Home*, published by Help the Aged (address on p 114), is full of practical advice about different aspects of home safety.

▶ **The Royal Society for the Prevention of Accidents** (ROSPA – address on p 117) produces books and leaflets about home safety.

▶ **Your local council** will probably have someone who can advise about home safety. Try the environmental health department or the housing department, or ask for the occupational therapist in the social services department.

5 Making a long-term decision

This chapter looks at the long-term decisions you and your relative may have to make about how she will be cared for. If she has been seriously ill or injured, she may no longer be able to manage living at home, even with care and support.

Before any decisions are made, your relative and other members of the family will want to talk through the options. If your relative lives with someone, the decisions will obviously affect them too. It is worth taking time to think about all the issues, and making sure everyone is involved.

It is important to involve someone from social services, too, as they will be able to tell you what is realistically possible in the area where your relative lives, and what is not. A lot may also depend on how much money you and your relative have.

When talking through the options, it is worth bearing in mind that your relative's condition may well change and the decision you make may therefore not turn out to be a final one.

‘Many people have no choice. But we did have the choice, and for us it just seemed the right thing to do.’

Rosemary's mother was very independent and capable until she was 91. Then she had a series of minor strokes which left her feeling confused and agitated. The doctor said she should no longer live on her own. Rosemary suggested she should come and stay on a temporary basis while they decided what to do.

'My brother and his wife came over from Manchester, and we all sat down and discussed what would be best. Our son was away at college, and our daughter had already decided she wanted to go and get a flat of her own with some friends. So although we only have a three-bedroom house, room was no problem. What's more my husband had just retired from his job, so he would be there to give me a hand. My brother and his wife were both still working full-time, but they could have her to stay from time to time to give us a break.

'Many people have no choice about caring for a relative, and I don't want to pass any judgements. But we did have the choice, and for us it just seemed the right thing to do.

'We did our best to make her feel at home, by bringing things from her house and putting them in her room. She had a Welsh dresser she was fond of, and we brought that and put it downstairs. In fact after she'd been with us a while she seemed to forget all about her own home.

'Mother did once go into a nursing home for a fortnight, while we had a holiday. But she wasn't happy there. It's not that they didn't look after her. On the contrary, perhaps they did too much for her, because we noticed there were things she'd been able to do for herself that she could no longer cope with.'

Rosemary has no regrets about the three years she spent caring for her mother.

'I'm not saying it was always a picnic. But we could see she was happy with us. Her friends would come and visit. The vicar used to drop in. We would all laugh and joke. It felt natural. Now that she's died, we all feel glad she was with us until the end. In fact it was a joy.'

What are the options?

Before coming to any decision, you and your relative and the rest of the family will want to look at all the possible options. Looking through the seven options for your relative listed below could be a good starting point, although the options listed are obviously not exhaustive.

1 She could **carry on living in her own home**, but with more help and support, and maybe some alterations to make her home more suitable.

2 She could **move into sheltered housing** or some other kind of housing with support.

3 She could **move to live near you** or another family member.

4 You or another family member could **move to live near her**.

5 She could **move in with you** or another family member.

6 You or another family member could **move in with her**.

7 She could **move into a residential or nursing home**.

In each case there are of course many different ways things could be organised, depending on your relative's individual circumstances.

The advantages and disadvantages of each option are discussed on pages 67–71.

Can your relative live independently?

The first thing for you and your relative to decide is whether she can live on her own (or with another person such as a spouse or friend), provided she gets enough help. If the answer is yes, you could consider options 1, 2, 3 or 4. If the answer is no, and you and your relative feel she needs more care than can be provided if she lives on her own, you could consider options 5, 6 or 7. Even if it seems that your relative will be able to go on living on her own, the situation may change if her condition becomes worse.

If you are not sure, ask the social services department to make an assessment of your relative's needs (see pp 19–21). You might find it helpful to talk to her GP or the district nurse or the consultant who looked after her if she has been in hospital.

NOTE: If you and your relative decide that moving into a residential or nursing home is the best option, but she needs help with the costs, you should talk to a social worker. Under the 1990 NHS and Community Care Act, the local social services department can help with care home costs only if they consider that your relative *needs* residential or nursing home care and cannot be cared for in the community. For more about paying for residential or nursing home care, see pp 82–83.

Advantages and disadvantages of the different options

Option 1 Your relative carries on living in her own home

Advantages

May be what your relative wishes.

Independence retained.

Familiar surroundings.

Less upheaval.

Friends and neighbours close by.

Possible disadvantages

Risk of further illness or injury (your relative may be willing to accept some risk if she wants to stay at home).

Not enough help available.

Loneliness (especially if your relative is housebound).

Family possibly too far away to visit frequently.

Things to look into

The long-term outlook for your relative's health (see pp 44–58).

Support services at home (see pp 26–29).

Adapting the home (see pp 29–32).

Option 2 Your relative moves into sheltered housing

(Sheltered housing is described on pp 72–75.)

Advantages

Independence retained.

Risk may be less if alarm system or warden on site.

Purpose-built housing: easy to look after, all on the same level.

No need to make alterations to existing home.

Possibly some communal facilities.

Possible disadvantages

Unfamiliar surroundings.

Upheaval of moving.

Nuisance of having to sell present home.

Expense: depends on housing scheme, and whether buying or renting.

Possible waiting list.

Not available, or only available in wrong area.

Things to look into

Sheltered housing schemes in the area (contact the council's housing department).

Support services at home (see pp 26–29).

Option 3 Your relative moves to live near you

Advantages

Independence retained.

Family close by.

Possible disadvantages

Unfamiliar surroundings.

Upheaval of moving.

Loss of contact with friends and neighbours.

Difficulty of finding suitable place.

What happens if you have to move to a different area?

Things to look into

Sheltered housing schemes in the area (contact the council's housing department).

Support services at home (see pp 26–29).

Adapting the home (see pp 29–32).

Option 4 You move to live near your relative

Advantages

Independence retained.

Familiar surroundings.

Less upheaval.

Family and friends close by.

Possible disadvantages

Upheaval for you and your family.

Financial implications if you have to give up work.

You may lose contact with your own support network.

Difficulty of finding suitable place.

Things to look into

Housing and employment possibilities in the area you are thinking of moving to.

Support services at home (see pp 26–29).

Adapting the home (see pp 29–32).

Option 5 Relative moves in with you

Advantages

Less risk if someone is always or often there.

Your relative may like to be cared for by her own family.

Companionship for your relative.

Possible disadvantages

Loss of independence for your relative.

Upheaval of moving.

Stress for you and your family: you may feel you have no life of your own.

Possible friction and bad feeling between you and your relative.

Your home may not be suitable.

Things to look into

Support services at home (see pp 26–29).

Adapting the home (see pp 29–32).

Legal and financial considerations arising out of sharing a property (see *Housing Options for Older People*, published by ACE Books – details on p 122).

Option 6 You move in with your relative

Advantages

Familiar surroundings.

Less upheaval.

Friends and neighbours close by.

Your relative may like to be looked after by her own family.

Possible disadvantages

Loss of independence for your relative.

Upheaval for you and your family.

Stress for you and your family: you may feel you have no life of your own.

Possible friction and bad feeling between you and your relative.

Your relative's home may not be suitable.

Financial implications if you have to give up work.

Things to look into

Support services at home (see pp 26–29).

Adapting the home (see pp 29–32).

Legal and financial considerations arising out of sharing a property (see *Housing Options for Older People*, published by ACE Books – details on p 122).

Option 7 Your relative moves into residential or nursing home

(Residential and nursing home care is described on pp 75–83.)

Advantages

Safety: someone is always there.

Round-the-clock care.

Good facilities.

Possible companionship.

Less disruption for you.

Possible disadvantages

Loss of independence.

Unfamiliar surroundings.

Loss of contact with family, friends, neighbours.

Your relative may feel unwanted and unloved.

Family may feel guilty.

Expense: if your relative has savings over £8,000, or social services do not think she *needs* residential care, she may have to pay the full cost (see pp 82–83).

Difficulty of finding a place in a home that will accept someone with your relative's disability.

Difficulty of finding a home your relative likes.

Things to look into

Residential and nursing homes in the area (contact the local social services department).

Talking things over

With so many different needs and views to take into account, talking through the options can be more difficult than you would think. It may help if you are aware of some of the possible sources of misunderstanding. You may then be able to smooth over disagreements, or present things in a different way which makes them easier to understand.

These are just some of the ways misunderstandings can arise:

▶ Your relative, or other members of the family, may be confused and not really understand the options.

▶ Your relative may want to avoid upsetting anyone, and this may lead her to say different things to different members of the family, or go along with other people's suggestions.

▶ Your relative may change her mind but not feel able to say so because she feels under pressure.

▶ Your relative may resist some options because she feels she is being rejected.

▶ Different members of the family may have strong feelings about what should happen. Your relative may feel under pressure to agree to suggestions, even if the pressure is not deliberate.

▶ Your relative may believe she is going to die soon, so there is no point in making any arrangements. Or other members of the family may think this. But no one will voice this thought.

▶ Different people may be given different information by health and social services staff.

▶ People may feel torn between conflicting emotions such as love, guilt and resentment, other commitments, even financial considerations. There may be hidden resentments between family members.

Sheltered housing

Sheltered housing is special housing for older people or people with disabilities who are fairly independent, but want the security of having someone there to keep an eye on them. Most sheltered housing is in purpose-built developments of flats (and sometimes bungalows), which are rented from the local council or a housing association. Often there is a resident warden on site, but sometimes there is a mobile warden who keeps an eye on a number of sheltered housing schemes.

Another advantage of sheltered housing is that the units are quite small and easy to heat and look after. They are usually all on one level, though not always on the ground floor, so if this is important for your relative, you should check that a bungalow or ground floor flat is available.

There are many different kinds of sheltered housing scheme, providing different levels of warden service. In some schemes, the warden is there all the time, and may also arrange for shopping, home help/home care and other services. In other schemes, the warden just drops in daily or once in a while to check that residents are all right. All other arrangements have to be made individually by the residents.

How to find out more about renting sheltered housing

The best way to find out about sheltered housing in your area is to contact the local council's housing department to ask if they could consider an application. If not, they may be able to send you a list of housing associations which have sheltered housing in the area.

The main thing taken into account when a council or housing association considers applications is the person's housing need at the time they apply. The amount of time spent on a waiting list may be immaterial.

Many housing associations allocate 50 per cent or even 100 per cent of their properties to people nominated by the local council. To nominate someone, the council must be satisfied that they are a 'high priority' for sheltered housing.

Sheltered housing to buy

In some areas, there are private sheltered housing schemes where you can buy a unit, either from a housing association or from a private company. It is very important, if you are thinking of buying into one of these schemes, to find out exactly what is included in the purchase price, and what extras there are. You should check what regular outgoings there will be, for example for heating, service charges, maintenance, cleaning, gardening, water rates, Council Tax, etc. You may find that the weekly outgoings are almost as much as paying rent.

Abbeyfield houses

Abbeyfield houses are another popular alternative. These are large houses with bedsits for up to about ten older people, and a resident housekeeper. Meals are provided, which means the cost may be a little higher than in ordinary sheltered housing. For some people, Abbeyfield houses offer the best of both worlds, combining privacy and independence with social and practical support. They are usually more suitable for fairly active and independent people, but some Abbeyfield houses now provide care for more dependent people. You can get more information about schemes in your area from the address on page 107.

Sheltered housing checklist

▶ What exactly are the warden's responsibilities? Do they meet your relative's needs? Is there relief cover when the warden is not on duty?

▶ What arrangements can be made for other care services, for example home help/home care, visits from district nurse or GP, meals on wheels, hairdressing, chiropody?

▶ Is the flat/bungalow accessible? Does your relative need to be on the ground floor? Is it all on one level inside?

▶ Is the flat/bungalow big enough? Is there room for your relative's furniture? Is there sufficient storage space?

▶ What facilities are there in each flat/bungalow? If your relative has a disability, is the flat/bungalow suitable? Does it have any special adaptations, for example wide doors, wheelchair ramps, internal lifts, grab-rails by the entrance doors and in the bathroom and toilet, waist-level sockets, lever taps, easily opened windows, a walk-in shower?

▶ Are there any communal facilities, for example a social room, TV lounge, laundry facilities, shared garden area?

▶ Are there visitors' rooms, so friends and relatives can come to stay?

▶ What are the other people who live there like? Do you think your relative will get on with them? Are there any organised social activities or outings?

▶ Are pets allowed?

▶ Is there a policy about smoking in communal areas?

▶ How much does it cost to live there? And what does the rent include? What about repairs, heating, water rates, Council Tax, TV licence? Are there any hidden extras you need to know about?

FOR MORE INFORMATION

▶ Age Concern England Factsheet 2 *Sheltered housing for sale.*

▶ Age Concern England Factsheet 8 *Rented accommodation for older people.*

▶ Age Concern England Factsheet 9 *Rented accommodation for older people in Greater London.*

▶ Age Concern England Factsheet 24 *Housing schemes for older people where a capital sum is required.*

▶ Help the Aged Information Sheet 2 *Sheltered Housing.*

▶ *Housing Options for Older People*, published by ACE Books (details on p 122).

Residential or nursing home care

For some people, care in a residential or nursing home might be the best answer. **Residential homes** are for people who need help with personal care. **Nursing homes** are for people who need nursing care as well. They are usually rather more expensive, because they employ qualified nursing staff.

Making a decision about moving into a care home is never easy, because it is such a big step for anyone to admit they can no longer manage on their own. If you and your relative are not sure whether she needs residential or nursing home care, you can ask the social services department of your council to carry out an assessment (see pp 19–21).

In the past some homes had rather a bad name, and many people are still reluctant to consider this alternative for their relatives. Nowadays homes are closely supervised, and many people are very satisfied with the care they get.

Private and voluntary residential homes for four or more elderly people are required by law to be registered with the local authority and inspected by them at least twice a year. The local social services department will therefore have its own Inspection Unit which checks up regularly on homes on its list. If you are not happy with something in the home, and you cannot resolve it by talking to the staff, you should let the Inspection Unit know.

All nursing homes have to be registered with the District Health Authority and inspected at least twice a year; they must be run by a qualified doctor or nurse.

However, it is still important, if only for your own peace of mind, to take great care in choosing a home for your relative.

NOTE Small residential homes, for less than four people, are registered under a simplified process, and may not be regularly inspected, so it is up to you to look into them carefully and rely on your own judgement.

MARGARET

❝By this time I was so desperate I would have taken almost anything.❞

'Mum suffered from Parkinson's disease, and my father looked after her. When he telephoned to ask me to call the doctor, I knew something was wrong. I jumped in my car and drove the 250 miles to where they lived. By the time I got there, the doctor had arrived, and he had called an ambulance. Dad had had a heart attack, and Mum was dehydrated and confused. The doctor arranged for them both to be admitted to hospital.

'After about a fortnight, the hospital started to pressure me to remove Mum. They said there wasn't anything more they could do for her. Dad was still in hospital, so I went down to fetch her. I put Mum and the cat in the car, and brought them up here. Mum was disorientated and confused. She wanted to go home. She just wanted things to be as they had been before.'

Margaret arranged for her mother to see a geriatric consultant at the local hospital, where she was diagnosed as having Alzheimer's disease and admitted for three weeks while her medication was sorted out. But the weekend she was discharged, there was a phone call from the hospital in the south saying Margaret's father was seriously ill.

'We tried to find someone to look after Mum. The social services department couldn't help us – they told us to contact Crossroads. But before they could sort it out, Dad died. I'll always regret that I wasn't able to see him before he died.'

Margaret found looking after mother increasingly stressful. She thought about giving up her job, but decided against it because her husband's job was not secure. The children found their eccentric grandmother difficult to live with, too.

'It was a very hard time for the whole family. She couldn't be left on her own. She needed someone there all the time, in case she did anything dangerous. But then she always picked arguments. We'd never had an easy relationship, but now I was just finding it impossible. The whole family was under stress. In the end, it was the geriatric consultant who said she would be better off in a home. He told us about a new residential home that had just opened. It wasn't perfect, but they were friendly and kind. Mother was delighted.'

At first Margaret's mother seemed happy, but as her illness progressed she became listless and depressed, and wouldn't eat. After a year, the home could no longer cope. Margaret would have to find a nursing home that could give her mother more care.

'Social services gave us a list of homes. Most of them were full, or couldn't take people as ill as my mother. Nobody gave me any help or advice. I felt as though everything was up to me. I visited one home that was rather up-market, but the atmosphere was cold. There seemed to be no one about. The second one seemed very shabby and crowded. I was beginning to despair. In fact I think by this time I was so desperate I would have taken almost anything. Then I remembered another home that was a bit further away that I sometimes passed on my way from work. We went to visit, and we liked it at once. It had a good atmosphere, and they had a place. I was so relieved.

'When I visit Mum she seems much happier. Sometimes she tells me outrageous things, but then I realise she's confusing it with the boarding school she went to as a child. I do feel guilty sometimes – I feel I've copped out. But I also know we had no choice.'

How social services can help

If the social services department assesses your relative and decides she cannot manage in her own home, and needs to be in a residential or nursing home, they may arrange a place for her. This could be a council-run residential home, a private home, or one run by a voluntary organisation or charity. If your relative's capital assets are £8,000 or below, they will also cover all or part of the cost, as explained on pages 82–83.

If you want a different home to the one suggested by social services

You and your relative may prefer a different home to the one the council offers. You may, for example, prefer your relative to be in a home close to where you live. There should be no problem about this, so long as the owners of the home are prepared to make a contract with the council, but if the home costs more than the council usually pays, you may have to make up the difference.

The council should not, however, set an arbitrary limit to what they are prepared to pay. They should pay the full cost of a place to meet your relative's assessed needs. If you are not satisfied with what the council offers – for example, you feel she *needs* to be somewhere where her family can visit her easily and they have offered a place 50 miles away – you can make a complaint, using the social services department complaints procedure. All social services departments must now have one.

Choosing the right home

You should be able to get a list of registered residential homes from the social services department of your local council, and a list of registered nursing homes from the District Health Authority. Ask at the local hospital, or ring the main number for your health authority and ask who you should speak to. You could also contact the local Age Concern office, the Community Health Council or the Citizens Advice Bureau. Many residential and nursing homes advertise in local newspapers and of course in the *Yellow Pages*. Some of the organisations listed at the end of this section can also help with information about homes.

It is not easy to choose a home for another person. The things which matter to your relative may not be the things which seem most important to you, so it is helpful if you can talk together about what you are looking for in a home. If your relative is severely mentally disabled, this may not of course be possible, and you will have to make the decision on your own or with other members of the family.

In some areas, it may not be easy to find a home with a vacancy. Some homes are reluctant to take very frail or ill people, for example people who have suffered a severe stroke. Some homes are unwilling to take residents with severe symptoms of dementia, especially if they have undergone personality changes which make them difficult or aggressive.

If you have difficulty in finding a place in a home, you may feel so grateful when you do find one that you make the mistake of accepting the first one that is offered. If you cannot find a home that will accept your relative, you may find it helpful to contact Counsel and Care or the Elderly Accommodation Council (addresses on pp 111 and 112). You should speak to her social worker if she has one.

If at all possible, it is a good idea to visit a number of homes – even if they don't have current vacancies – so that you can make comparisons, and be confident that the home you choose for your relative is right for her.

If the home is well run, they will not mind you asking a lot of questions. They will be pleased that you are concerned for your relative.

Residential and nursing home checklist

Does the home meet your relative's needs?

▶ Does it take people with your relative's illness/disability?

▶ Does it provide the right level of care (for example nursing care if necessary)?

▶ Is it in a convenient place for you to visit regularly?

▶ If your relative is in a wheelchair, is there good wheelchair access to all parts of the building?

▶ Is the building all on one level, or is there an internal lift?

▶ If your relative needs special treatment or a special diet, will the home be able to provide it?

▶ What will happen to your relative if her condition deteriorates or improves?

▶ Is there a vacancy? How long is the waiting list?

▶ Is it possible for your relative to stay in the home for a **trial period** of say a week or two, to see whether it suits her? (Many homes now offer this.)

Is the home well run?

▶ Are there sufficient trained staff?

▶ What staff are in the home at night?

▶ Is the home properly insured and inspected?

▶ Is it clean? Is it homely? Are there plants and flowers around? Are there any pets?

▶ What is the food like? Is there a choice? How large are the portions?

▶ How do the staff seem to behave towards the residents?

▶ What happens if a resident has a complaint?

Does the home encourage residents to be independent?

▶ Are residents encouraged to do things for themselves and make decisions for themselves as much as possible?

▶ Can residents be involved in everyday activities such as cleaning, cooking, gardening, looking after pets?

▶ Do residents usually look after their own money? What are the arrangements if they are not able to?

▶ Does the home respect residents' need for privacy? Do staff knock before going into a resident's room?

▶ Can residents prepare food and drinks in their own rooms?

▶ Can residents sometimes eat privately with their guests?

▶ Can residents see visitors when and where they choose?

▶ Is there a telephone residents can use for incoming and outgoing calls where they can talk in privacy?

▶ Can residents decide for themselves when to go to bed and when to get up in the mornings? If not, are you happy with the arrangements?

▶ What are the arrangements for handling medicines? Do residents have a say in this?

▶ Can residents see their own doctor, or is there one doctor who sees all the residents in the home?

▶ Does the home let residents have a say about how things are run? Is there a residents' committee?

What are the facilities like?

▶ Are the rooms single or shared? If your relative has to share a room, is there any choice about who she shares with?

▶ Will your relative be able to reach a toilet easily, both from her own room and from the dining room and other shared areas?

▶ Is there more than one living room, so that there is a quiet room as well as a television room?

▶ What is the policy about smoking? Are there smoking and non-smoking areas?

Will your relative be happy there?

▶ Are the other residents the sort of people she could get on with and make friends with?

▶ Will your relative be able to keep any personal possessions in her room, such as pictures, plants, flowers, furniture?

▶ If your relative is physically active, will there be enough activities apart from watching television to keep her busy?

▶ Are there up-to-date books, newspapers and magazines for residents? Does a mobile library visit, or can residents go to the local library?

▶ Are there any organised activities residents can get involved in? Does the home take residents out on trips and visits, for example shopping, or to the theatre or cinema, or to a place of worship?

▶ If your relative likes gardening, is there any opportunity for her to be responsible for an area of garden?

How much will it cost?

▶ How much is the weekly fee? What exactly does it cover?

▶ What are the extras? Ask about hairdressing, chiropody, extra drinks or snacks, incontinence supplies, special diet, newspapers, a television or telephone in your relative's own room, trips and outings, treatments such as physiotherapy, speech therapy or massage (if relevant to your relative), and any other services you think your relative will need. (Residents or their visitors will usually be expected to buy things for personal use such as clothes, toiletries, stationery, etc.)

▶ Do you have to pay a deposit on booking? Is it refundable?

- If the home puts up its fees, how much notice will you get?

- If your relative is away from the home for a short time, for example in hospital or on holiday, what fees will she still have to pay?

- Is there a contract to sign? Who has to sign it – the person staying in the home, or another family member? (If you are asked to sign a contract on behalf of your relative, you should seek legal advice from a solicitor or the Citizens Advice Bureau about what exactly you are committing yourself to.)

- How much notice will you have to give if your relative leaves the home?

- What happens about payment if your relative dies while she is in the home?

Paying for residential or nursing home care

Residential and nursing homes can be very expensive, but if your relative's capital assets are £8,000 or below she may get help with the cost. The rules about paying for residential and nursing home care are extremely complicated. They are explained in detail in the free Age Concern Factsheet No 10 *Charging procedures for residential and nursing home care*. The following information is just for guidance to give you a rough idea of the position.

Savings

Anyone who has savings or investments over £8,000 will have to pay the full cost of residential or nursing home care (unless care is arranged by the health authority, in which case the health authority pays the full cost of the place).

If your relative owns a house or flat, its value could be counted as part of her savings. However, this does not apply if she is only going to be in a care home temporarily, or if her spouse or another 'relative' who is aged 60 or over or is disabled still lives there. The local authority has discretion to ignore the value of the home when someone else lives there.

Even if your relative starts by paying the full cost, she can apply to the council as soon as her savings drop down to £8,000. This could happen quite quickly. Don't wait until she has no savings left at all. Ask for an early assessment if your relative's savings will soon reach £8,000.

Income

All your relative's income (minus a small allowance for personal expenses) must go towards the cost of the home. The social services department then pays the balance.

NOTE If you find all this confusing, don't worry. The social services department will work it out for you. For extra help and advice, contact your nearest Citizens Advice Bureau or the local Age Concern organisation. If you are not satisfied, you can make a complaint through the social services department complaints procedure.

Still not decided?

Balancing everybody's needs and wishes is never easy. Remember *there is no perfect solution*. Whatever option you and your relative choose, there are bound to be times when you regret it and feel you have made the wrong decision. The important thing is to be happy in your own mind that you and your relative considered all the options and made the best decision in the circumstances.

FOR MORE INFORMATION

▶ Age Concern England Factsheet 10 *Local authority charging procedures for residential and nursing home care*.

▶ Age Concern England Factsheet 29 *Finding residential and nursing home accommodation*.

▶ Help the Aged (address on p 113) Information Sheet 10 *Residential and Nursing Homes*.

▶ Factsheet from Counsel and Care (see below) *What to look for in a private or voluntary registered home*.

▶ **Counsel and Care** (address on p 111) is a voluntary organisation which gives advice and information about voluntary and private residential and nursing homes. They may be able to help if you have difficulty in finding a place in a home.

▶ **The Relatives' Association** (address on p 117) provides support and advice for the relatives of people who are in long-term residential or nursing home care.

6 Money matters

If your relative becomes very ill, physically or mentally, you may need to take steps to take over the running of her affairs. Even if your relative's illness is not too prolonged, you may well need to arrange to collect her pension and other benefits for her. If she is ill for a long time – or she is not likely to recover – you (or another family member) will probably need to take over the running of her affairs more completely. Obviously you will do this with your relative's consent if she is capable of understanding what she is doing; if she is not, you may have to take over without her consent. This chapter explains how you do this.

It also looks at some of the benefits that may be available either to your relative or to you as a carer, so that you can check that you and your relative are claiming any benefits you are entitled to.

Finally, this chapter explains why it is important to make a Will and how to go about making one. If your relative becomes very ill and has not made a Will, she may want you to help her make one – or you may want to try to persuade her that it is a good idea.

MANINDER

Maninder's mother suffered from Parkinson's disease, and was cared for by her husband. She became increasingly confused after her husband died. Eventually she was diagnosed as having Alzheimer's disease, and the geriatric consultant said she should be in a nursing home. Maninder realised that she would now have to sell her parents' house.

'We contacted a solicitor, and he said something about enduring power of attorney. But they messed us about for such a long time drawing up the document that by the time it was ready it was too late. Mum's confusion had returned, and she couldn't sign it. So we had to go through the whole business of obtaining the forms from the Court of Protection and getting a doctor to complete one of them certifying that she was mentally unsound, and not capable of making her own decisions. The forms then had to be returned to the Court and eventually a Receivership Order was issued, which enabled me to sell the house and handle her affairs. That took six months.'

The house was then placed with an estate agent, and fortunately it was sold quite quickly. The Court of Protection gave instructions as to where the money should be invested.

'I have to account for every penny I spend. The first year was a nightmare, when there were all sorts of small expenses like the newspaper bill and the milkman to pay off. Now it's settled more into a routine. I have to keep records and receipts of all expenditure – her nursing home fees, the occasional shopping trip, Christmas and birthday presents, and so on.

'The worst thing is the lack of information from the Court of Protection. They tell me about my obligations as a receiver – like having to fill in her tax return, submit annual accounts and pay an annual fee – but I don't seem to have any rights – not even the right to information.

'I wish I'd known earlier about enduring power of attorney. Then we could have avoided all this.'

Taking over responsibility for someone's affairs

Collecting pension and other benefits

Provided your relative is still mentally competent – that is, capable of understanding what she is doing – she can nominate you or another relative to collect her State Pension and any other benefits from the post office. If the situation is a temporary one, you and your relative simply need to complete and sign the form on the back of the order. If the situation is likely to continue for some time, you can get an agency card from the Benefits Agency (social security) office.

If your relative is not capable of understanding what she is doing, the Benefits Agency can name you or another close relative as her appointee to claim and collect benefits on your relative's behalf.

Using bank and building society accounts

If your relative is physically unable to get to the bank or building society, she may authorise you to use her account. This is known as a 'third party mandate'.

Power of attorney

This is a document which gives someone the legal right to manage another person's affairs, for example if they are ill in hospital or away on holiday. An **ordinary** power of attorney only applies so long as the person giving it is mentally competent.

Enduring power of attorney

An enduring power of attorney remains valid even if the person giving it later becomes mentally incapable. But it *must* be created by someone who is mentally capable at the time.

This can be a good idea if your relative is getting more forgetful and absent-minded, and you think she may soon become incapable of managing her affairs. You may be worried that she is beginning to suffer from dementia. This is not an easy subject to discuss with your relative, and for this reason many people avoid it until it is too late. If talking about creating an enduring power of attorney causes such bad feeling that it could poison your relationship, it may be better to leave it.

An enduring power of attorney may appoint you to take over your relative's affairs at once and to continue if she becomes mentally incapable in the future, or it may appoint you to take over her affairs only if she becomes mentally incapable. Some people draw up an enduring power of attorney that will come into effect only under certain conditions, for example their doctor diagnoses them as having dementia. You could discuss these conditions with your relative, and write them into the agreement. Sometimes people do this at the same time as making their Will, as a way of preparing for the future.

As soon as you believe your relative is becoming or has become unable to manage her affairs or to supervise your actions, the enduring power of attorney *must* be registered with the Court of Protection. Once the Court of Protection has registered the document and sent it back to you, you can show it to the bank, building society, etc, if you want to withdraw money or carry out other transactions. (If the enduring power of attorney permits you to take over your relative's affairs at once, you should do this immediately.) However, there are still rules laid down by the Court of Protection about how you can spend the money.

You can buy a special document to create a power of attorney from a legal stationer, or you can ask a solicitor to draw one up for you. A useful booklet is *Enduring Power of Attorney*, available free from the Court of Protection.

Applying to the Court of Protection

If your relative becomes mentally incapable of managing her own affairs before she has given someone else enduring power of attorney, you may need to apply to the Court of Protection for authorisation to manage her money. If a person has assets of more than £5,000, the Court usually appoints and supervises a **receiver** to manage their affairs. This could be a member of the family, or it could be a professional person such as a social worker or solicitor. The Court charges an annual fee for supervising the receiver's activities.

If your relative's estate (money, property and other assets) is simple and straightforward, or is worth less than £5,000, the Court may issue a Short Procedure Order (instead of a Receivership Order) authorising you to use her assets in a certain way for her benefit.

Applying to the Court of Protection is costly and complicated, so it is better to avoid it if you can by encouraging your relative to create an enduring power of attorney in good time.

FOR MORE INFORMATION

▶ *Enduring Power of Attorney* and *Handbook for Receivers*, available free from the Court of Protection. Send a large sae to the address on page 111.

▶ Age Concern England Factsheet 22 *Legal arrangements for managing financial affairs*.

▶ *Managing Other People's Money*, published by ACE Books (details on p 123).

▶ *Enduring Power of Attorney* by Stephen Cretney, published by Jordans.

▶ *Making the Most of the Court of Protection,* edited by David Carsons, published by the King's Fund.

▶ *Court of Protection Handbook* by Norman Whitehorn, published by Longman.

▶ To find out more about the Court of Protection, or to make an application, contact them at the address on page 111.

Welfare benefits, pensions and tax

Being ill or disabled may prove very expensive for your relative, particularly if she has to pay for care. You, too, may find all kinds of unexpected claims on your budget, from paying someone to do the garden because you are too busy to do it to contributing towards the costs of care services for your relative. It is therefore worth making sure that both you and your relative are claiming any benefits you may be entitled to.

The welfare benefits system is quite complicated, and claiming everything you are entitled to can be difficult and time-consuming. You do not have to be an expert to claim benefits, but it certainly helps to have some idea of what you are entitled to, and possibly someone who *is* an expert to advise you. The Citizens Advice Bureau or another local advice centre is a good place to start. Some councils have specially trained staff in the social services department.

This section also looks very briefly at pensions – it is always worth checking that your relative is claiming all the pensions that are due to her and that she is not paying more Income Tax than she should be.

ROSEMARY

❝I found out about Attendance Allowance completely by chance from the girl in the village post office.❞

Rosemary's mother came to live with Rosemary and her husband when she was 91, after a series of minor strokes which left her feeling confused and agitated. Rosemary looked after her mother for the next three years, until she died. Rosemary has no regrets about caring for her mother, but she does feel angry that she was never told about the benefits her mother could claim.

'I found out about Attendance Allowance completely by chance from the girl in the village post office. We realised she could have been claiming it for two years, but nobody told us. It was the same with the Poll Tax. A friend I met at church told me that elderly mentally disabled people didn't have to pay. Otherwise we would never have known.'

After her last stroke Rosemary's mother became much more confused, needing care during the night as well as during the day. They applied for the higher level of Attendance Allowance, which covers day and night-time care.

'We were told she would have to wait six months. I think that's very niggardly. If she needs care now, why should she have to wait six months to get the allowance?

'Then when she became incontinent she was given special stretch pants to wear over her pads. We were allowed just two pairs per year. Just imagine how long two pairs would last for someone who was doubly incontinent. This penny-pinching attitude makes me cross, when you think of how much more it would cost them if we weren't looking after her. But I suppose that's political!'

▶ If you are not sure whether there is a benefit you or your relative could claim, explain the situation and ask if there is help available.

▶ If you think you or your relative could be entitled to a benefit but you are not sure, you can always claim anyway: you have nothing to lose.

▶ Make your claim as soon as possible. Some benefits cannot be backdated before the date when you first claim.

▶ If you or your relative have been refused a benefit you think you are entitled to, don't be afraid to appeal.

▶ Get an 'expert' to help you make your claim or appeal.

Benefits for people with a disability

Attendance Allowance

This is a weekly allowance paid to people over the age of 65 who become ill or disabled. It is meant to help with the cost of being looked after, though it is up to the person how they actually spend the allowance.

To qualify for Attendance Allowance people must need help with personal care (washing, dressing, eating, going to the toilet, etc), supervision, or to have someone watching over them.

Attendance Allowance is paid at two rates. The lower rate is for people who need care either during the day or at night. The higher rate is for people who need care both during the day and at night.

A person must usually have been disabled for six months before they can get the allowance, but someone who is terminally ill can be paid it straight away.

Attendance Allowance does not depend on National Insurance contributions, nor is it affected by income or savings. People do not pay tax on it, and it does not affect other social security benefits.

Disability Living Allowance

Disability Living Allowance (DLA) has replaced Attendance Allowance and Mobility Allowance for people who become disabled under the age of 65. There is a 'care component', paid at three different levels according to how much looking after people need, and a 'mobility component', paid at two different levels according to how much difficulty they have in moving about.

Like Attendance Allowance, DLA does not depend on NI contributions and is not affected by income or savings. It is tax-free, and can be paid on top of other benefits.

Other benefits your relative may be able to claim

Statutory Sick Pay (SSP) Paid by the employer instead of wages for the first 28 weeks to someone who is too sick or disabled to work.

Sickness Benefit Paid to people who are too sick or disabled to work but who do not qualify for SSP, perhaps because they are unemployed or self-employed. It lasts for 28 weeks, and depends on NI contributions, except in cases of industrial disease or injury.

Invalidity Benefit For people of working age who have been too sick or disabled to work for over 28 weeks. It depends on NI contributions, except if you were disabled as the result of an industrial disease or accident.

Severe Disablement Allowance For people of working age who are too sick or disabled to work but who cannot claim Sickness or Invalidity Benefit because they have not paid enough NI contributions.

Disability Working Allowance For people with disabilities who are employed but are only able to earn low wages because of their disability.

Industrial Injuries Disablement Benefit An extra allowance for people who became sick or injured through their work.

Pneumoconiosis, byssinosis and miscellaneous disease benefits For people who contracted an industrial disease before 5 July 1948.

Constant Attendance Allowance A weekly allowance for people very severely disabled through their work or a war injury.

FOR MORE INFORMATION

▶ Age Concern England Factsheet 18 *A brief guide to money benefits*.

▶ *Your Rights*, published annually by ACE Books (details on p 123), a comprehensive guide to money benefits for older people.

▶ DSS leaflet FB 2 *Which Benefit?* explains most benefits and tells you how to claim.

► For information about any benefit, ring the Benefits Agency Freeline 0800 666 555 (9.30 am–4.30 pm weekdays).

► For information about disability benefits you could also ring the Benefits Enquiry Line 0800 882 200 (9.30 am–4.30 pm weekdays).

Benefits for carers

Invalid Care Allowance

Invalid Care Allowance (ICA) is the only benefit specially for carers. It is for people of working age who cannot work full-time because they are looking after someone. You may qualify for ICA if you meet the following conditions:

► You look after someone for at least 35 hours a week.

► You do not earn more than a certain amount (£50 in 1993–94).

► You are aged below 65 when you first claim.

► The person you care for receives Attendance Allowance, the higher or middle levels of the **care** component of Disability Living Allowance, or Constant Attendance Allowance.

ICA is counted as income if you are getting a means-tested benefit such as Income Support, Housing Benefit or Council Tax Benefit, or if someone is claiming a benefit for you. It is not paid on top of most other benefits. But it may still be worth claiming, as it entitles you to the carer premium, paid as part of Income Support, Housing Benefit and Council Tax Benefit (see pp 93–94).

NOTE If your relative receives the severe disability premium with Income Support, Council Tax Benefit or Housing Benefit, she will lose this if you claim Invalid Care Allowance for yourself. If in doubt, ask the Citizens Advice Bureau to calculate whether it's sensible for you to claim.

The carer premium

This is not a benefit in itself, but an extra amount of money paid to someone who is getting Income Support, Housing Benefit or Council Tax Benefit. You will be entitled to the carer premium if you are entitled to Invalid Care Allowance (even if you don't get ICA because you are already getting other benefits).

▶ DSS leaflet FB 31 *Caring for Someone?* describes benefits for carers and for disabled people.

▶ Leaflet 4 *Invalid Care Allowance: What it is, Who can get it, How to claim it* and Leaflet 5 *Invalid Care Allowance, National Insurance, Income Tax and Other DSS Benefits*, available free from the Carers National Association. Send a large sae to the address on page 109.

Benefits for people with low incomes

Income Support

Income Support helps with basic living expenses by topping up people's weekly income to a level set by the Government. The exact level is announced in November each year. It is means-tested – which means that income and savings are taken into account. People with savings of over £8,000 do not qualify, and people with savings of between £3,000 and £8,000 get a reduced amount (1993–94 figures). People with children, single parents, pensioners, and sick or disabled people get an extra amount.

Someone caring for a disabled person may also get an extra amount, called the carer's premium (see p 92).

Help with the costs of residential or nursing home care

People on a low income may be able to get Income Support to help with the costs of a private or voluntary residential or nursing home. For more information about paying for residential or nursing home care, see pages 82–83.

Housing Benefit

Housing Benefit helps with the cost of rent for people with a low income, and savings of £16,000 or less. You or your relative may qualify for some Housing Benefit even if you do not qualify for Income Support. You will be sent a claim form automatically if you are on Income Support. If not, apply to your local council.

Help with the Council Tax

The Council Tax is a new local tax, introduced in April 1993, replacing the Community Charge (Poll Tax). It is based on the value of your house. People may be helped with the Council Tax in various ways:

▶ People who have a low income may qualify for Council Tax Benefit, claimed in the same way as Housing Benefit.

▶ If someone living with you (not your partner or a lodger) has a low income, you may qualify for 'second adult rebate', which is part of the Council Tax Benefit scheme.

▶ People living on their own get a discount of 25 per cent. Adults who are 'severely mentally impaired' and some carers are not counted as an extra person.

▶ People with disabilities may get a reduction if their house has certain special features.

The Social Fund

The Social Fund makes lump-sum payments to people with low incomes to help with exceptional expenses.

Cold Weather Payments and **Funeral Payments** are mandatory (they must be made if you fulfil the qualifying conditions), and **Community Care Grants**, **Budgeting Loans** and **Crisis Loans** are all discretionary. Budgeting Loans and Crisis Loans have to be paid back but they are interest-free.

These payments are mainly available to people on Income Support, but people who receive Housing Benefit or Council Tax Benefit may qualify for Funeral Payments.

Free prescriptions, dental treatment, eye tests and vouchers for glasses

There are different rules for different NHS treatments. People on Income Support or low incomes may be entitled to treatment free or at a reduced cost, as may people with certain conditions or disabilities. Ask your doctor, dentist or optician, or get hold of the Benefits Agency booklet *Help With Health Costs*.

► Age Concern England Factsheet 25 *Income Support and the Social Fund*.

► Age Concern England Factsheet 16 *Income-related benefits: Income and capital*.

► Age Concern England Factsheet 17 *Housing Benefit and Council Tax Benefit*.

► Age Concern England Factsheet 21 *The Council Tax and older people*.

► Age Concern England Factsheet 5 *Dental care in retirement*.

► For information about any benefit, ring the Benefits Agency Freeline 0800 666 555 (9.30 am–4.30 pm weekdays). They are very helpful, and they don't ask any personal questions.

Pensions

As well as checking that you and your relative are claiming any benefits you may be entitled to, it is worth checking that your relative is collecting any pensions that are due to her.

State Basic Pension

Most people who have worked get a Basic Pension from the State when they retire. The exact amount they get depends on how many National Insurance contributions they have paid during their working life. Married women, widowed people and divorcees who do not qualify for a full Basic Pension may be able to claim a pension based on their spouse's contributions. Women who worked during the war may also be entitled to a small pension.

Other pensions your relative may be entitled to

Additional Pension, paid under the State Earnings-Related Pension Scheme (SERPS), based on earnings since 1978.

Graduated Pension, based on earnings between April 1961 and April 1975.

Over-80s Pension for people over 80 who do not get the full State Basic Pension.

An occupational or personal pension.

Tax allowances

It is also worth checking that your relative is claiming all the tax allowances she is entitled to. A tax allowance is the amount of income you are allowed to receive without paying any Income Tax. There are special tax allowances for people aged 65 and over, and for registered blind people. If you think your relative may be entitled to an extra tax allowance, contact the tax office (Inland Revenue) for your area.

FOR MORE INFORMATION

For more information about the State Retirement Pension see:

▶ DSS leaflet NP 46 *A Guide to Retirement Pensions*.

▶ Age Concern England Factsheet 20 *National Insurance contributions and qualifying for a pension*.

▶ *Your Rights*, published annually by ACE Books (details on p 123).

If you have a problem with an occupational pension that you cannot sort out with your employer or pension provider, contact:

▶ **Occupational Pensions Advisory Service** (OPAS – address on p 116).

For more information about tax see:

▶ Age Concern England Factsheet 15 *Income Tax and older people*.

▶ *Your Taxes and Savings*, published annually by ACE Books (details on p 123).

Making a Will

Making a Will tends to be something that people put off, because they find it upsetting to think about death. If your relative has not made a Will, you may find raising the subject of making one extremely hard, especially if she has a terminal illness. But in fact it may put her mind at rest if she can talk about what will happen to her money and property when she dies. You could ask, 'Have you thought about what you would like to do about . . . ?' You could even suggest making a Will yourself to make it all seem more everyday. You could ask other people who have been in the same position for advice about how to broach the subject tactfully.

A Will makes it easier for the relatives to carry out someone's wishes after they die. The Will names one or more people to be the **executors**: this means they will be responsible for sorting out the dead person's money and property (their **estate**) and carrying out the instructions in the Will. The executor is usually a surviving spouse or other close relative, but it could be a professional such as a solicitor or bank manager. A professional executor will usually charge a fee, which is paid out of the estate.

Getting help with making a Will

It is best to ask a solicitor to help in drawing up a Will, especially if your relative's financial or family situation is at all complicated. The fees solicitors charge can vary a great deal, from about £35 to £200, so it may be worth ringing up a few solicitors and asking for a quotation. If there is a family solicitor who has looked after the family's affairs for a number of years, you may prefer to go to them.

Some people draw up their own Wills. The Consumers' Association has a Will pack and has published a guide called *Wills and Probate* which tells you how to draw up your own Will. Age Concern England has also produced a useful factsheet. It is important that the Will is clear, and that it is dated, signed and witnessed in the right way. Otherwise it will not be valid. The witnesses to the signature cannot be beneficiaries or their spouses; the executor can be a beneficiary.

What happens if there is no Will?

If a person dies without making a Will, or the Will is not valid, this is called dying **intestate**. If this happens, the personal representative of the person who has died (usually their closest surviving relative) may need to go to the Probate Registry office and ask for the papers to allow them to handle the dead person's affairs. The address of the Probate Registry office will be in the local telephone book.

The property will be divided up according to a strict set of rules. These are explained in the DSS booklet *What to Do After a Death*, available free of charge from your local Benefits Agency (social security) office. The rules of intestacy are complicated, and the personal representative may need to seek legal advice before dividing up the estate.

If your relative has got married or divorced since she made her Will, the Will is usually not valid, so she will need to make a new one.

FOR MORE INFORMATION

▶ DSS booklet D 49 *What to Do After a Death*.

▶ Age Concern England Factsheet 7 *Making your Will*.

▶ Age Concern England Factsheet 14 *Probate: Dealing with someone's estate*.

▶ *Wills and Probate, What to Do When Someone Dies* and *Will Pack*, all published by the Consumers' Association (address on p 110).

7 If the person you are looking after dies

If, despite all your efforts and all the arrangements you have made, your relative dies, this will undoubtedly come as a great shock. You may feel a rush of different emotions which are almost overwhelming: panic, grief, fear, loss, relief, guilt, anger, regret, loneliness, to name but a few.

If your relative dies in hospital, the staff will take care of the practicalities, and you may have some space to begin to come to term with your own feelings.

If you are with your relative at home as she approaches death, you will probably be doing all you can to make her feel comfortable, and you may not have time to think about your own feelings until afterwards.

A feeling of panic often arises after someone has died because you feel you ought to be doing something, but you have no idea at all what you should do. This section gives you a step-by-step guide to all the practical things that need to be taken care of when someone dies.

❝I was with her when I realised she was dying.❞

'When my mother-in-law was admitted to hospital, they told her the operation was for her thyroid. Cancer was never mentioned.

Nobody ever talked about death or dying. Everyone kept jollying her along, saying "Are you all right?" and things like that. I think I was the only one she could admit it to.

'I was with her when I realised she was dying. I had my three-year-old son with me. He kept saying, "Why doesn't Granny say Hello?" I didn't want him to be there, but I didn't know what to do. Fortunately a neighbour came round at that point, and I was able to take him away and leave him at a relative's house.

'By the time I got back, the doctor had been and had given her an injection, so she died peacefully.'

Things to do at once

1 Don't panic

Before you do anything else, take a deep breath and try to calm your-self down. You could try some of the tips for keeping calm listed on pages 9–10. You may want to make sure that your relative has died by checking her pulse, or holding a mirror to her lips, or seeing if there is any reaction in her eyes. But don't worry if you can't do this – the doctor will check when he or she arrives.

2 Call the doctor

If the GP has been looking after your relative through her illness, and knows the cause of death, he or she will confirm that she has died, and issue a medical certificate giving the cause of death. You must give this to the registrar when you go to register the death (see point 8 below). The GP should also give you a leaflet explaining how to register the death.

If your relative is to be cremated, you will need an extra form signed by a different doctor. The funeral director or the GP will arrange this. The Will should be read to see if it contains any instructions about the funeral, and the executor should be consulted before any funeral arrangements are made.

Sometimes, if the doctor has not seen the person who has died in the last 14 days, or would like to know more about the cause of death, he or she will report the death to the coroner. The coroner may then arrange for a post mortem examination. This usually happens when the person has died from an unknown cause, from an accident or injury, or from an industrial disease. The coroner may also order a post mortem if the person died during an operation, or under anaesthetic. There is nothing to be worried about if this happens, and there should be no delay in the funeral arrangements.

3 If your relative wanted to be an organ donor

More and more people now choose to donate organs from their body when they die. If you think your relative would have liked this, or if she carried an organ donor card, then contact the nearest hospital as soon as you can, so that the organs can be removed quickly. Heart, liver or lung donations are usually only taken from people under 60 who died in hospital and were on a ventilator. Kidneys may be donated up to about the age of 75, but they must be removed within 24 hours of death. Corneas, bone and skin are sometimes accepted from even older people.

If your relative wished her whole body to be used for research, contact the medical school of the nearest teaching hospital.

4 Contact a funeral director

As soon as you have the medical certificate from the doctor, you can go ahead and contact a funeral director. The funeral director will help you decide about the practical arrangements for the funeral, such as:

► Will your relative be buried or cremated? (Some people express a wish about this before they die.) There are some extra forms to be filled in if a person is to be cremated. The funeral director will tell you about these.

► Would you like the body to be kept at home or in a chapel of rest until the funeral?

► Will there be a funeral service or other non-religious ceremony? (If so, you need to contact the people involved.)

► Would you prefer people to send flowers or make donations to a charity?

It is important to choose a funeral director you feel comfortable with. You can get names of local funeral directors from the *Yellow Pages* of the telephone directory, or you can ask friends and neighbours whom they would recommend. Funerals can be very expensive, so don't be afraid to ask for two or three written estimates before you decide, and make sure you are clear what is included and what is extra. The difference between estimates could well be considerable. Choose a funeral director who is a member of the British Institute of Funeral Directors or the National Association of Funeral Directors (addresses on pp 108 and 115).

Some people like to choose a funeral director and discuss arrangements in advance of death. This may seem gloomy, but if death is not far away, then having the arrangements made in advance means there will be one less thing to worry about at the time. The British Institute of Funeral Directors can send you a leaflet called *Taking Care of the Future*, which explains how to arrange a funeral in advance.

People who receive certain State benefits may be able to get help with the cost of a funeral from the Social Fund, as explained on page 94. You should also check among your relative's documents to see whether she has paid for her funeral in advance.

5 Contact close relatives and friends

It is a good idea to contact relatives and friends as soon as possible. They can give you comfort and support in this difficult time, and they may be able to help you with some of the arrangements.

6 Contact the minister of religion

If your relative belonged to a religion then contact the minister. Even if she did not attend a place of worship, she may have wanted a religious funeral. Many people become more religious as they grow older.

7 Washing and laying out the body

Whether you do this depends very much on your own feelings. In the past, it was usually done by members of the family, but nowadays it is often done by the district nurse or the funeral director.

Things to do over the next few days

8 Register the death

When someone dies, their death must be registered with the Registrar of Births, Deaths and Marriages for your area. You must do this within five days. You will find the address in the local telephone directory.

You should show the registrar:

▶ the medical certificate given you by the GP;

▶ the pink form (Form 100) given you by the coroner (if the death was reported to the coroner);

▶ your relative's medical card and war pension order book, if she had one.

The registrar will also want to know:

▶ your relative's full name, and her maiden name if it was different;

▶ the date and place of death;

▶ her last permanent address;

▶ where and when she was born;

▶ what her occupation was;

▶ whether she was receiving a State Pension or other benefits;

▶ if she was married, the date of birth of the surviving spouse.

The registrar should give you:

▶ a green certificate for burial or cremation. You should give this to the funeral director: burial or cremation cannot take place without it;

► a white certificate of registration of death, used for claiming social security benefits.

If there is a surviving widow, she should also obtain information leaflets about widow's benefits and Income Tax from the registrar's office.

The registrar will only give you a death certificate if you ask for one. There is a small charge for this. You may need a death certificate for sorting out the Will, or to claim pension and insurance rights.

9 Sort out the Will

The person named in the Will as the executor is the person responsible for dealing with the money, property and possessions owned by the person who has died. After all debts have been settled, the estate is distributed in accordance with the dead person's Will. If you are feeling upset, this may be the last thing you feel like doing. You may find it helpful to go to a solicitor or the Citizens Advice Bureau.

The executor may need to obtain a **grant of probate** from the Probate Registry office (listed in your local telephone directory) to allow them to collect all the assets and carry out the instructions in the Will.

If there is no Will, someone acting as the dead person's **personal representative** may need to obtain **letters of administration** from the Probate Registry office instead. This will depend on the value of the estate, and whether institutions such as National Savings, building society and bank are willing to release the assets without letters of administration.

For information about how to do this, and about how to settle the estate once you have obtained probate, see the publications listed on page 105.

If there is an executor named in a Will or an administrator appointed in letters of administration, the following tasks should be left to that person.

10 Return personal documents and NHS equipment

Personal documents such as pension book, passport, driving licence, cheque book and credit cards should be returned to the offices which issued them.

Don't forget to return any NHS equipment on loan to your relative, such as a wheelchair, commode or hearing aid.

11 Dispose of personal belongings

Some people find it very distressing to sort through and dispose of the belongings of someone who has died. If possible, do this with other family members or close friends. You will be able to share your memories of your relative, and you are less likely to end up throwing away some memento which someone else would have treasured.

Many charities are pleased to accept the personal belongings of someone who has died, or you may like to give them away to family and friends. Some firms specialise in clearing out the homes of people who have died. They usually advertise in the local newspapers in the 'Wanted' section. But be warned, they often end up making a tidy profit out of antiques and other items whose value people do not realise.

FOR MORE INFORMATION

▶ Age Concern England Factsheet 27 *Arranging a funeral.*

▶ Age Concern England Factsheet 14 *Probate: Dealing with someone's estate.*

▶ DSS booklet D 49 *What to Do After a Death.*

▶ DSS leaflet *How to Obtain Probate.* Available from the Registrar of Births, Deaths and Marriages.

▶ *Wills and Probate* and *What to Do When Someone Dies*, published by the Consumers' Association (address on p 110).

Your feelings when someone close to you dies

Everyone has their own way of saying goodbye to someone they were close to. It is usually better to let yourself feel all the painful emotions that come to the surface at this time, rather than thinking you have to show control. Most people feel grief and a sense of loss; but it is not unusual to feel guilt, anger, bitterness, resentment and other negative feelings as well. Sometimes these difficult and contradictory emotions take us by surprise, and they can make us think there is something 'wrong' with our feelings for the person who has died. In fact grieving is a very personal process, and the feelings we go through, although they may follow a similar pattern, will be different for everybody. There is no 'right' or 'wrong' way of mourning – there is just a way which works for you, and helps you come to terms with your loss.

If you are feeling so unhappy that you just cannot cope, you should be able to get professional help. Your GP is the first person to go to. You may be able to get in touch with a bereavement counsellor through your GP or through a hospice or hospital.

There are also some voluntary organisations which support bereaved people. CRUSE – Bereavement Care (address on p 111) is an organisation which helps bereaved people. It has local branches in some areas. Phone the national office or look in your local telephone directory. Compassionate Friends offer support if you have lost a child, and the Lesbian and Gay Bereavement Project if you have lost a partner or your friend or relative has died of AIDS (addresses on pp 110 and 114).

The National Association of Bereavement Services (address on p 115) will be able to put you in touch with a bereavement counsellor in your area.

If you are feeling seriously depressed, your GP may refer you to the community psychiatric nurse or put you in touch with a psychotherapist or psychiatrist. MIND (address on p 114) also offers and advises about counselling and psychotherapy.

FOR MORE INFORMATION

▶ *Bereavement*, a short leaflet which explains the grieving process, and gives you advice about how to get help. Produced by the Royal College of Psychiatrists, 17 Belgrave Square, London SW1X 8PG. Tel: 071-235 2351.

▶ *Through Grief* by Elizabeth Collick, a book about bereavement available from CRUSE (address on p 111).

▶ *Understanding Bereavement*, an advice leaflet available from MIND Publications (address on p 114).

Abbeyfield Society
Housing association specialising in
bedsits for older people in shared
houses with meals provided.

186–192 Darkes Lane
Potters Bar
Hertfordshire EN6 1AB
Tel: 0707 644845

Action for Dysphasic Adults
Help and information about dysphasia
(loss of language).

1 Royal Street
London SE1 7LL
Tel: 071-261 9572

AIDS helplines
Freephone: 0800 567 123 (English – 24 hours)
0800 282 445 (Asian – Wednesday 6–10 pm)
0800 282 446 (Cantonese – Wednesday 6–10 pm)
0800 282 447 (Arabic – Wednesday 6–10 pm)
0800 521 361 (Minicom service for deaf people – daily 10 am–10 pm)
0800 555 777 (Health Literature Line – 24 hours)

Alzheimer's Disease Society
Information, support and advice
about caring for someone with
Alzheimer's disease.

Gordon House
10 Greencoat Place
London SW1P 1PH
Tel: 071-306 0606

Arthritis and Rheumatism Council for Research
Information about all aspects of
these diseases.

PO Box 177
Chesterfield
Derbyshire S41 7TQ
Tel: 0246 558033

Arthritis Care
Advice about living with arthritis,
loan of equipment, holiday centres.
Local branches in many areas.

18 Stephenson Way
London NW1 2HD
Tel: 071-916 1500

Association of Charity Officers
Advice about how to find out about charities which could help you.

c/o RICS
Benevolent Fund Ltd
1st Floor
Tavistock House North
Tavistock Square
London WC1H 9RJ
Tel: 071-383 5557

Association of Crossroads Care Attendant Schemes
See Crossroads Care

BACUP (British Association of Cancer United Patients)
Support and information for cancer sufferers and their families.
Freephone advice line for people outside London: 0800 181 199.

3 Bath Place
Rivington Street
London EC2A 3JR
Tel: 071-696 9003

British Association for Counselling
To find out about counselling services in your area.

1 Regent Place
Rugby
Warwickshire CV21 2PJ
Tel: 0788 578328/9

British Association of the Hard of Hearing
See Hearing Concern

British Heart Foundation
Information about all aspects of heart disease.

14 Fitzhardinge Street
London W1H 4DH
Tel: 071-935 0185

British Institute of Funeral Directors
Information about arranging a funeral, and about funeral directors in your area.

146a High Street
Tonbridge
Kent TN9 1BB
Tel: 0732 770332

British Lung Foundation
Information about all aspects of lung disease.

8 Peterborough Mews
London SW6 3BL
Tel: 071-371 7704

British Red Cross
Loans home aids for disabled people.
Local branches in many cities.

9 Grosvenor Crescent
London SW1X 7EJ
Tel: 071-235 5454

Calibre
Free cassette library for blind people.

Aylesbury
Buckingham HP22 5XQ
Tel: 0296 432339/81211

Cancer Relief Macmillan Fund
Can put you in touch with Macmillan nurse service in your area.

Anchor House
15–19 Britten Street
London SW3 3TZ
Tel: 071-351 7811

CancerLink
Information and advice about all aspects of cancer.

17 Britannia Street
London WC1X 9JN
Tel: 071-833 2451

Care Alternatives – Care for the Elderly
A private agency which provides care for elderly people in their own homes. Mainly London area, but can arrange live-in care nationwide.

206 Worple Road
London SW20 8PN
Tel: 081-946 8202

Care and Repair
Advice about home repairs and improvements.

Castle House
Kirtley Drive
Nottingham NG7 1LD
Tel: 0602 799091

Carematch
Computerised information about residential care for people with physical disabilities.

286 Camden Road
London N7 0BJ
Tel: 071-609 9966

Carers National Association
Information and advice if you are caring for someone. Can put you in touch with other carers and carers' groups in your area.

20–25 Glasshouse Yard
London EC1A 4JS
Tel: 071-490 8818
Special Adviceline:
071-490 8898 (1–4 pm weekdays)

London Region

5 Chalton Street
London NW1 1JD
Tel: 071-383 3460

Scotland

11 Queens Crescent
Glasgow G4 9AS
Tel: 041-333 9495

NW Yorkshire and Humberside Region

Chalton House
Salem Church
36 Hunslet Road
Leeds LS10 1JN
Tel: 0532 449228

Caresearch
*Computerised information on
residential and respite care for people
with learning disabilities.*

c/o Janet Hepburn
Fairways
St Briavels
Lydney
Gloucester GL15 6SQ
Tel: 0594 530220

Centre for Accessible Environments
*Information for architects and
builders about designing homes for
people with disabilities. Also register
of architects with experience of this.*

35 Great Smith Street
London SW1P 3BJ
Tel: 071-222 7980

Chest Heart and Stroke Association
See Stroke Association, British Heart Foundation and British
Lung Foundation

Citizens Advice Bureau
*For advice on legal, financial and
consumer matters. A good place to
turn to if you don't know where to go
for help or advice on any subject.*

Listed in local telephone
directories, or in *Yellow
Pages* under 'Counselling
and advice'. Other local
advice centres may also
be listed.

Coloplast Foundation
*Help and advice for people who
have had a colostomy.*

Coloplast Advisory Service
FREEPOST
Peterborough Business Park
Peterborough PE2 6BR
Freephone: 0800 622 124
Stoma Care Freephone:
0800 220 622

Community Health Council
*For enquiries or complaints about
any aspect of the NHS in your area.*

See the local telephone
directory for your area
(sometimes listed under
District Health Authority).

Compassionate Friends
Comfort if you have lost a child.

53 North Street
Bristol BS3 1EN
Tel: 0272 539639

Consumers' Association
*Publishes regular reports and full-length
books on many different goods and
services.*

2 Marylebone Road
London NW1 4DX
Tel: 071-486 5544

**Consumers' Association
Book Sales Dept**

Castlemead
Gascoyne Way
Hertford SG14 1LH
Tel: 0992 589031

Continence Foundation
*Advice and information about whom
to contact with incontinence problems.*

The Basement
2 Doughty Street
London WC1N 2PH
Tel: 071-404 6875

Counsel and Care
*Advice for elderly people and their
families; can sometimes give grants to
help people remain at home, or return
to their home.*

Lower Ground Floor
Twyman House
16 Bonny Street
London NW1 9PG
Tel: 071-485 1566

Court of Protection
*If you need to take over the affairs of
someone who is mentally incapable.*

Public Trust Office
Protection Division
Stewart House
24 Kingsway
London WC2B 6JX
Tel: 071-269 7157/7358/7317

Crossroads Care
*For a care attendant to come into your
home and look after your relative.*

10 Regent Place
Rugby
Warwickshire CV21 2PN
Tel: 0788 573653

CRUSE – Bereavement Care
*Comfort in bereavement. Can put you
in touch with people in your area.*

126 Sheen Road
Surrey TW9 1UR
Tel: 081-940 4818/9047

Department of Social Security (DSS)
Formerly DHSS. Welfare rights and benefits section is called the
Benefits Agency. Phone Freephone 0800 666 555 or see your local
telephone directory.

**Dial UK (Disablement Information
and Advice Lines)**
*Information and advice for people
with disabilities. Can put you in
touch with local contacts.*

Park Lodge
St Catherine's Hospital
Tickhill Road
Balby
Doncaster DN4 8QN
Tel: 0302 310123

**Dial-a-Ride and Taxicard Users'
Association (DART)**
*Information about dial-a-ride and
taxicard services in your area.*

St Margaret's
25 Leighton Road
London NW5 2QD
Tel: 071-482 2325

Disability Alliance Education and Research Association
Campaigns for a better deal for people with disabilities; information about welfare benefits.

1st Floor East
Universal House
88–94 Wentworth Street
London E1 7SA
Tel: 071-247 8776
Welfare rights enquiries:
071-247 8763

Disability Law Service
Free legal advice for disabled people and their families.

16 Princeton Street
London WC1R 4BD
Tel: 071-831 8031/7740

Disabled Car Purchase
(formerly Assistance and Independence for Disabled People – AID)
Advice about buying a car or having your car adapted.

114 Commonwealth Road
Caterham
Surrey CR3 6LS
Tel: 0883 345298

Disabled Drivers' Association
Information and advice for disabled drivers.

Ashwellthorpe Hall
Norwich
Norfolk NR16 1EX
Tel: 050-841 449

Disabled Drivers' Motor Club
Information and advice about mobility problems for disabled people, whether they are drivers or passengers.

Cottingham Way
Thrapston
Northants NN14 4PL
Tel: 0832 734724

Disabled Living Centres Council
Can tell you where your nearest Disabled Living Centre is, where you can see and try out aids and equipment.

286 Camden Road
London N7 OBJ
Tel: 071-700 1707

Disabled Living Foundation
Information about aids to help you cope with a disability.

380–384 Harrow Road
London W9 2HU
Tel: 071-289 6111

Elderly Accommodation Council
Computerised information about all forms of accommodation for older people and advice on top-up funding.

46a Chiswick High Road
London W4 1SZ
Tel: 081-995 8320/742 1182

Family Health Services Association
The body responsible for GPs and primary health care.

See your local telephone directory.

Forces Help Society
Help for ex-service people and their families; runs residential homes.

122 Brompton Road
London SW3 1JE
Tel: 071-589 3243

Greater London Association for Disabled People (GLAD)
Information for disabled people in the London area.

336 Brixton Road
London SW9 7AA
Tel: 071-274 0107

Headway (National Head Injuries Association)
For people who are disabled physically or mentally as a result of a head injury, and their carers.

7 King Edward Court
King Edward Street
Nottingham NG1 1EW
Tel: 0602 240800

Health Education Authority (HEA)
Leaflets and advice about many aspects of health care.

Information Centre
Hamilton House
Mabledon Place
London WC1H 9TX
Tel: 071-383 3833

Hearing Concern
Information and support for people with hearing loss.

7–11 Armstrong Road
London W3 7JL
Tel: 081-743 1110/1353

Help the Aged
Advice and information for older people and their families.

16–18 St James's Walk
London EC1R OBE
Tel: 071-253 0253
Winter Warmth
Hotline/Seniorline:
0800 289 494

Holiday Care Service
Free information and advice about holidays for elderly or disabled people and their carers.

2 Old Bank Chambers
Station Road
Horley
Surrey RH6 9HW
Tel: 0293 774535

Hospice Information Service
Information about local hospices which care for people who are terminally ill.

St Christopher's Hospice
51–59 Lawrie Park Road
Sydenham
London SE26 6DZ
Tel: 081-778 9252

Incontinence Information Helpline
Information and advice about managing incontinence, and how to contact your nearest continence adviser.

Tel: 091-213 0050

Jewish Care
Social care, personal support,
residential homes for Jewish people.

Stuart Young House
221 Golders Green Road
London NW11 9DQ
Tel: 081-458 3282

John Groom's Association for the Disabled
Residential, respite and holiday
accommodation.

10 Gloucester Drive
Finsbury Park
London N4 2LP
Tel: 081-802 7272

Leonard Cheshire Foundation
Residential homes and home care
attendants for disabled people.

26–29 Maunsel Street
London SW1P 2QN
Tel: 071-828 1822

Lesbian and Gay Bereavement Project
Counselling, advice and support for
lesbians, gay men, and their families
and friends.

Vaughan M Williams Centre
Colindale Hospital
London NW9 5HG
Tel: 081-200 0511
(3–6 pm weekdays)
Helpline: 081-455 8894
(7 pm–midnight)

London Accessible Transport Unit (LATU)
Advice about transport for disabled
people in the London area.

Britannia House
1–11 Glenthorne Road
London W6 OLF
Tel: 081-741 8363

Marie Curie Memorial Foundation
Nursing care and advice for
cancer patients.

28 Belgrave Square
London SW1X 8QG
Tel: 071-235 3325

MENCAP (Royal Society for Mentally Handicapped Children and Adults)
Advice and support for people caring
for someone with a learning disability.

National Centre
123 Golden Lane
London EC1Y ORT
Tel: 071-454 0454

MIND (National Association for Mental Health)
Information, support and
publications about all aspects of
mental illness, depression, etc.

22 Harley Street
London W1N 2ED
Tel: 071-637 0741

MIND Publications Mail Order Service

1st Floor
Kemp House
152–160 City Road
London EC1V 2NP
Tel: 071-608 3752

Mobility Advice and Vehicle Information Service (MAVIS)
Advice for disabled car drivers.

Department of Transport Research Laboratory
Old Wokingham Road
Crowthorne
Berkshire RG11 6AU
Tel: 0344 770456

Motability
Cars and wheelchairs for disabled people.

2nd Floor
Gate House
Westgate
Harlow
Essex CM20 1HR
Tel: 0279 635666

National Association of Bereavement Services
Information about bereavement and loss counselling services in your area.

20 Norton Folgate
London E1 6DB
Tel: 071-247 1080
(24-hour answerphone)

National Association of Councils for Voluntary Service
Can tell you how to find your local CVS, which puts volunteers in touch with people needing help.

3rd Floor
Arundel Court
177 Arundel Street
Sheffield S1 2NU
Tel: 0742 786636
(Or look in your telephone directory for the local Council for Voluntary Services.)

National Association of Funeral Directors
Offers code of conduct and a simple service for a basic funeral.

618 Warwick Road
Solihull B91 1AA
Tel: 021-711 1343

National Association of Patient Participation Groups
Can put you in touch with patient participation groups in your area.

11 Hardie Avenue
Moreton
Wirral
Merseyside L46 6BJ
Tel: 051-677 9616

National Council for Voluntary Organisations (NCVO)
Information about voluntary organisations in your locality which could be a source of help.

Regents Wharf
8 All Saints Street
London N1 9RL
Tel: 071-713 6161
(Or look in your telephone directory: there may be a local Council for Voluntary Organisations.)

National Head Injuries Association
See Headway

National Schizophrenia Fellowship (NSF)
Information about schizophrenia.

28 Castle Street
Kingston upon Thames
Surrey KT1 1SS
Tel: 081-547 3937

National Self Help Support Centre
Information about local self-help groups and how to set one up.

Regents Wharf
8 All Saints Street
London N1 9RL
Tel: 071-713 6161

Network for the Handicapped
See Disability Law Service

Occupational Pensions Advisory Service (OPAS)
For queries and problems to do with occupational pensions that you cannot sort out with your employer or pension provider.

11 Belgrave Road
London SW1V 1RB
Tel: 071-233 8080

Parkinson's Disease Society
Information and advice for people caring for someone with Parkinson's disease; many local branches.

22 Upper Woburn Place
London WC1H 0RA
Tel: 071-383 3513

Partially Sighted Society
Low Vision Advice Service
Advice, information and aids for partially sighted people.

62 Salusbury Road
London NW6 6NS
Tel: 071-372 1551

Pensioners Link
London only, but can put you in touch with similar groups in other areas.

405–407 Holloway Road
London N7 6HJ
Tel: 071-700 4070

RADAR (Royal Association for Disability and Rehabilitation)
Information about aids and mobility, holidays, sport and leisure for disabled people.

25 Mortimer Street
London W1N 8AB
Tel: 071-637 5400

Registered Nursing Homes Association
Information about registered nursing homes in your area.

Calthorpe House
Hagley Road
Edgbaston
Birmingham B16 8QY
Tel: 021-454 2511

Relate (formerly National Marriage Guidance Council)
Counselling and help with difficult relationships; many local branches.

Herbert Gray College
Little Church Street
Rugby
Warwickshire CV21 3AP
Tel: 0788 573241/560811

Relatives' Association
Support and advice for the relatives of people in a residential or nursing home or hospital long-term.

5 Tavistock Place
London WC1H 9SS
Tel: 071-916 6055/
081-201 9153

Richmond Fellowship
Therapeutic communities for people with or recovering from mental illness.

8 Addison Road
Kensington
London W14 8DL
Tel: 071-603 6373/4/5

Royal Association for Disability and Rehabilitation
See RADAR

Royal National Institute for Deaf People (RNID)
Information and advice about all aspects of hearing loss; information about hearing aids.

105 Gower Street
London WC1E 6AH
Tel: 071-387 8033

Royal National Institute for the Blind (RNIB)
Information and advice for blind people and their families.

224 Great Portland Street
London W1N 6AA
Tel: 071-388 1266

Royal Society for the Prevention of Accidents (ROSPA)
Leaflets about home safety.

Cannon House
The Priory
Queensway
Birmingham B4 6BS
Tel: 021-200 2461

St John Ambulance
Information about First Aid, and First Aid training.

1 Grosvenor Crescent
London SW1X 7EF
Tel: 071-235 5231

Samaritans
Someone to talk to if you are in despair.

See your local telephone directory.

Scottish Action on Dementia
For people caring for someone with dementia who live in Scotland.

8 Hill Street
Edinburgh EH2 3JZ
Tel: 031-220 4886

Scottish Council for Voluntary Organisations
For information about voluntary organisations in Scotland.

18–19 Claremont Crescent
Edinburgh EH7 4QD
Tel: 031-556 3882

Scottish Council on Disability
For people in Scotland who need advice or information about their disability.

Princes House
5 Shandwick Place
Edinburgh EH2 4RG
Tel: 031-229 8632

Self-Help Team
Information about self-help groups.

20 Pelham Road
Nottingham NG5 1AP
Tel: 0602 691212
(9.30 am–2.30 pm)

Shaftesbury Housing Association
Sheltered housing for elderly people.

18–20 Kingston Road
London SW19 1JZ
Tel: 081-542 5550

Soldiers, Sailors and Airmen Family Association (SSAFA)
Help for service or ex-service men and women and their families.

19 Queen Elizabeth Street
London SE1 2LP
Tel: 071-403 8783/
962 9696

Spinal Injuries Association
Information and advice for people who are disabled as a result of spinal injury.

Newpoint House
76 St James's Lane
London N10 3DF
Tel: 081-444 2121

SPOD (Association to Aid the Sexual and Personal Relationships of People with a Disability)

286 Camden Road
London N7 0BJ
Tel: 071-607 8851
Telephone counselling
Monday and Wednesday
1.30–4.30 pm and
Tuesday and Thursday
10.30 am–1.30 pm.

Standing Conference of Ethnic Minority Senior Citizens
Information, support and advice for older people from ethnic minorities and their families.

5 Westminster Bridge Road
London SE1 7XW
Tel: 071-928 0095

Stroke Association
Information and advice if you are caring for someone who has had a stroke.

123–127 Whitecross Street
London EC1Y 8JJ
Tel: 071-289 6111

Sue Ryder Foundation
Homes for disabled people.

Sue Ryder Homes
Cavendish
Sudbury
Suffolk CO10 8AY
Tel: 0787 280252

Talking Newspaper Association of the United Kingdom
Talking newspapers for blind and short-sighted people.

National Recording Centre
Heathfield
East Sussex TN21 8DB
Tel: 0435 866102

Tenovus
Emotional support and information on all aspects of cancer. Helpline answered by cancer-trained nurses and counsellors; available to everyone, but provides comprehensive bilingual service for the people of Wales.

Cancer Information Centre
142 Whitchurch Road
Cardiff CF4 3NA
Tel: 0222 619846
Helpline: 0800 526 527

Terence Higgins Trust
Information and advice about HIV/AIDS.

52–54 Gray's Inn Road
London WC1X 8JU
Tel: 071-831 0330
Helpline: 071-242 1010
(12 am–10 pm daily)

United Kingdom Home Care Association
Information about organisations providing home care in your area.

22 Southway
Carshalton
Surrey SM5 4HW
Tel: 081-770 3658

Wales Council for the Blind
Information and support for blind people and their families who live in Wales.

Shand House
20 Newport Road
Cardiff CF2 1YB
Tel: 0222 473954

Wales Council for the Deaf
*Information and support for deaf
people and their families who live
in Wales.*

Maritime Offices
Woodland Terrace
Maesycoed
Pontypridd
Mid Glamorgan CF37 1DZ
Tel: 0443 485687

Wales Council for Voluntary Action
*Information about voluntary groups
in Wales.*

Llys Ifor
Crescent Road
Caerphilly
Mid Glamorgan CF8 1XL
Tel: 0222 869224/86911

**Women's Royal Voluntary Service
(WRVS)**
*Provides meals at home for ill and
disabled people in some areas.*

234–244 Stockwell Road
London SW9 9SP
Tel: 071-416 0146

You might like to fill in your own **personal directory** on page 127.

About Age Concern

Caring in a Crisis: What to do and who to turn to is one of a wide range of publications produced by Age Concern England – National Council on Ageing. In addition, Age Concern is actively engaged in training, information provision, research and campaigning for retired people and those who work with them. It is a registered charity dependent on public support for the continuation of its work.

Age Concern England links closely with Age Concern centres in Scotland, Wales and Northern Ireland to form a network of over 1,400 independent local UK groups. These groups, with the invaluable help of an estimated 250,000 volunteers, aim to improve the quality of life for older people and develop services appropriate to local needs and resources. These include advice and information, day care, visiting services, transport schemes, clubs, and specialist facilities for physically and mentally frail older people.

Age Concern England
1268 London Road
London SW16 4ER
Tel: 081-679 8000

Age Concern Wales
4th Floor
1 Cathedral Road
Cardiff CF1 9SD
Tel: 0222 371566

Age Concern Scotland
54a Fountainbridge
Edinburgh EH3 9PT
Tel: 031-228 5656

Age Concern Northern Ireland
3 Lower Crescent
Belfast BT7 1NR
Tel: 0232 245729

A wide range of titles is published by Age Concern England under the ACE Books imprint.

Health and care

The Community Care Handbook: The new system explained
Barbara Meredith
The delivery of care in the community has changed dramatically as a result of recent legislation, and continues to evolve. Written by one of the country's foremost experts, this book explains the background to the reforms, what they are, how they operate, and who they affect.

£11.95 0–86242–121–7

Housing

Housing Options for Older People
David Bookbinder
A review of housing options is part of growing older. All the possibilities and their practical implications are carefully considered in this comprehensive guide.

£4.95 0–86242–108–X

An Owner's Guide: Your Home in Retirement
Co-published with NHTPC
This definitive guide considers all aspects of home maintenance of concern to retired people and those preparing for retirement, providing advice on heating, insulation and adaptations.

£2.50 0–86242–095–4

Money matters

Managing Other People's Money
Penny Letts
Foreword by the Master of the Court of Protection

The management of money and property is usually a personal and private matter. However, there may come a time when someone else has to take over on either a temporary or a permanent basis. This book looks at the circumstances in which such a need could arise and provides a step-by-step guide to the arrangements which have to be made.

£5.95 0–86242–090–3

Using Your Home as Capital
Cecil Hinton

This best-selling book for home-owners, updated annually, gives a detailed explanation of how to capitalise on the value of your home and obtain a regular additional income.

£4.50 0–86242–132–2

Your Rights: A guide to money benefits for older people
Sally West

A highly acclaimed annual guide to the State benefits available to older people. Contains current information on Income Support, Housing Benefit, Council Tax Benefit and Retirement Pensions, among other sources of financial help, and includes advice on how to claim them.

Telephone 081-679 8000 for more information.

Your Taxes and Savings: A guide for older people
Jennie Hawthorne and Sally West

This annual guide explains how the tax system affects older people over retirement age, including how to avoid paying more than necessary. The information about savings covers the wide range of investment opportunities now available.

For further information please telephone 081-679 8000

To order books, send a cheque or money order to the address below. Postage and packing are free. Credit card orders may be made on 081-679 8000.

ACE Books, Age Concern England, PO Box 9, London SW16 4EX.

Information factsheets

Age Concern England produces over 30 factsheets on a variety of subjects.

To order factsheets

Single copies are available free on receipt of a 9″ × 6″ sae. If you require a selection of factsheets or multiple copies totalling more than five, charges will be given on request.

A complete set of factsheets is available in a ring binder at the current cost of £34, which includes the first year's subscription. The current cost for annual subscription for subsequent years is £14. There are different rates of subscription for people living abroad.

Factsheets are revised and updated throughout the year and membership of the subscription service will ensure that your information is always current.

For further information, or to order factsheets, write to:

Information and Policy Department
Age Concern England
1268 London Road
London SW16 4ER

Index

geriatricians *40*
GPs *33, 38, 39*
grants: improvement *30–2*;
   see also benefits

health services *38–41*
health visitors *38, 39*
heart attacks *48–52*
heart failure *51*
home care organisers *19, 36*
home care workers, home helps *23, 36*
homes: adapting *27, 28, 29–32, 36–7, 42*;
   moving *68–70*; safety in *61–2*;
   staying in own *67*; support services
   26–9
homes, residential and nursing *25, 36, 71,*
   75–82; costs *67, 82–3, 93*
hospitals *12–13, 19, 38*; staff in *39–41*
housework, help with *26*
Housing Benefit *93*

improvement grants *30–2*
Income Support *93*
incontinence, help with *27, 39*
Invalid Care Allowance *92*
Invalidity Benefit *91*

laundry service *27*
leukaemia *34, 54*
link workers *25, 39*
luncheon clubs *27, 28*

Macmillan nurses *34, 41, 57*
meals on wheels *27, 36*
moving house *68–70*

neurologists *40*
nurses: agency *15*; community-based *27,*
   38, 39, 43; hospital-based *40–1*
nursing homes *see* homes, residential and
   nursing

occupational therapists (OTs) *19, 23, 24,*
   30, 36–7
oncologists *40*

ophthalmologists *40*
opticians *39, 94*
organs, donating *101*
orthopaedic surgeons *40*
osteoporosis *59*

pensions *95, 96, 104*; collecting someone
   else's *86*
physiotherapists *41, 53*
post mortems *101*
power of attorney *85, 86–7*
prescriptions, free *94*
psychiatrists *40*
psychogeriatricians *40*

residential homes *see* homes, residential
respite care *18, 28–9*
rheumatologists *40*

sheltered housing *68, 72–5*
shopping, help with *26, 28*
Social Fund *94*
social security *37*
social services *16, 17, 33, 35–7*;
   assessments *19–21, 24*; care
   managers *24–5, 37*; care plans *21–2*;
   complaints about *21, 22, 42*; dealing
   with *37, 41–2*; key workers *24, 37*
social workers *36, 38*
speech therapists *41*
Staying Put *30*
strokes *52–4*

tax allowances *96*
transient ischaemic attacks (TIAs) *52*
transport, help with *28*

urologists *40*

walking aids *27*
washing, help with *26, 36*
wheelchairs *27*
Wills *43, 96–8, 101, 104*

Personal directory

Fill in the phone numbers for your relative as soon as you can – provided that your relative is happy that you should have them – and keep in a safe place. It is unlikely that all these numbers will be relevant to your relative.

	Name/contact	*Telephone number*
Next-door neighbours		
Friends and relatives who live nearby		
GP		
District nurse		
Community psychiatric nurse		
Ambulance service		
Hospital (main switchboard)		
Hospital social worker		
Hospital occupational therapist		
Social services department (main switchboard)		

	Name/contact	Telephone number

**Social services
area team**

Social worker

**Key worker or
care manager**

**Social services
occupational therapist**

**Social services home
care organiser**

**Home care assistant
(home help)**

Personal care assistant

**Age Concern
(local branch)**

**Voluntary care
organisation**

Community transport

Church minister

Private care agency

Private nursing agency

**Council housing department
(main switchboard)**

**Local housing management
office (for council tenants)**

**Housing repair and
renovation grants**

Care and Repair

**Residential or
nursing home**

Other useful numbers